DECODING DOGS

WHAT'D YOU DO THAT FOR?

CASSIAN SANDEBERG
with LINDY KIRK

Decoding Dogs: What'd You Do That For?

Cassian Sandeberg

www.decodingdogs.com
www.birdhousepress.com
Published by Birdhouse Press
Los Angeles, CA 90035
www.BirdhousePress.com

Print ISBN: 978-0-99844-959-3
Print ISBN: 978-0-99844-958-6

Cover design by Eyerus

Printed in the United States of America.

This book is dedicated to everyone who has walked into a shelter or rescue and adopted a dog; to those who have pulled their car over, made a U-turn or slammed on their brakes to extend a helping hand to a stray; to anyone who has worked tirelessly to give a voice to the voiceless; and to the loyal owners of a challenging dog who have made sacrifices, determined to make that pet a loved and appreciated member of the family.

TABLE OF CONTENTS

ACKNOWLEDGEMENT

Thank you to Dakota Ladd and Jelani Yancey at Birdhouse Press for their hard work editing and proofreading this book.

Thank you to Renee Lawter and her team at Eyerus for creating a unique and eye-catching book cover.

And thank you to Duchess, my multi-issue dog who I've learned so much from over the years. And to Boomer, my canine assistant, who's helped me in the training of so many other dogs.

INTRODUCTION

"So what's going on?" I asked, taking a seat on the couch. Shooter, a handsome Australian Shepherd came sauntering up to me and I gave him a scratch behind his ears.

"Well," his dad began, adjusting awkwardly in his chair. "Shooter seems to have no sense of personal space."

I looked down at the dog who was lying at my feet. Typically, a dog with boundary issues would be nudging me for more attention or trying to crawl on my lap. "Really?" I asked, a bit confused.

Shooter's dad laughed. "Not all the time. Just in certain situations. Well, one certain situation, I guess."

"Which is?"

"When my girlfriend's over and we begin...getting close, he just loses it. He's all over us. And if we try to shut him out of the room, he goes crazy. Last night, after we...finished, I came out to find he'd peed in the hall and torn up a roll of toilet paper. All I could say was, 'What'd you do that for?!"

The following weekend I went to a session with a little yorkie named Petal and her mom. As soon as I walked into the apartment, my eyes were drawn to the walls. Covering nearly every inch were Post-It notes with affirmations scribbled on them. "You're beautiful," "Today is the day," "You can do anything you set your mind to," and so on. I walked from wall to wall, casually glancing at the notes while Petal's mom explained the issues.

"She just freaks out whenever I leave. My neighbors say she barks the entire time and whenever I come home, I always find something she's destroyed. She can't even stand it if I'm in a different room."

"How long have you had her?" I asked.

"About six months. I broke up with my boyfriend and needed a little companion." Right about then she noticed me reading the Post-It pep talks. "I know," she said with a laugh. "After my break up, I went through a pretty tough time. Petal was all I had. Up until last month we were never apart."

"And now?" I asked.

"Well, I used to work from home, but I just got a new job. So, I'm gone more during the weekdays. I'm also going out with friends more now."

For five months she served as her mom's security blanket, best friend and emotional support system. And not to say that her mom doesn't still love her and give her a great home, but a month ago things began to change. And Petal was never filled in on the new dynamic and expectations. One day she was her mom's entire world, and the next she was just one piece of the pie — expected to understand and adapt. Even though Petal couldn't talk, I heard her loud and clear, "What'd you do that for?!"

You may think the problem is your dog's inability to understand you, but I'm here to tell ya, it's a two-way street.

Does this sound familiar?

- Upon leaving the house, do you feel the need to give your dog Prozac – and maybe take one yourself?
- Is your pup a Velcro Dog, constantly clinging to your side, jumping on your lap and acting as your shadow?
- Do you find yourself dreading walks? Do you wrap the leash around your hand and wrist over and over again, as if preparing for battle, until you've lost all circulation?

- Are you going broke from buying the latest and greatest training gear?
- When you see another dog or person approaching, do you immediately search for a bush, alleyway or garbage can to jump into to avoid the impending Cujo reenactment?
- Are you becoming a hermit – refusing to leave your house or to allow visitors to enter?
- Do you lose your temper and shout at your dog so often you're beginning to think there may be a place for you guys on Jerry Springer's stage?
- Are you sending weekly letters to HGTV lobbying to get on one of their renovation shows in an attempt to repair all the damage your dog has caused?
- Have you strongly considered moving to a new city or state to avoid the angry stares and whispers of your neighbors?
- Do you feel the need to advise houseguests to bring an extra pair of pants with them to avoid embarrassment when your dog inevitably jumps up and rips the ones they're wearing?
- Do you feel as though you and your dog simply don't understand each other?

Did someone in your life buy you this book as a subtle hint that your beloved pup has an issue or two? Was it a friend? A neighbor? Perhaps your war-weary mailman left it on your front porch, sick and tired of buying new trousers and fearing for his life each time he approaches your house.

Or, perhaps you casually picked it up on your own accord, muttering to yourself, "This might be interesting. Not that *my* dog has issues or anything." But chances are, if you listen very closely, that little voice in the back of your mind is listing off certain behaviors or habits that may be less than desirable. Listen to that voice. If you ignore it, those unwanted behaviors will only persist, and possibly worsen.

And lastly, to those of you who dove headfirst into this book, seeking guidance, instruction, support and sanity, let me just say, I'm here to help. Sure, your dog may have some issues and maybe he's terrorizing the neighborhood children, but at least you've recognized it and you're taking responsibility.

Regardless of which category you fall into, the important thing to remember is, seeking help is not an admission of failure. In fact, I'm writing this book for all owners – even those with well-behaved pets. The goal here is to improve the dog-human relationship, no matter how rocky or stable it may be. This will not only improve your life, but also that of your dog.

It's important, as owners, that we understand the role we play in our dog's behavior; how our actions manifest within him and cause his reactions. For instance, some dogs can't handle just a little affection. You give them one rub and they just want more. If this sounds familiar, then take note and act accordingly. If he's lying down quietly, know what's to come if you give him a passing scratch behind the ear. Be conscious of your role — for every action, there's a reaction.

Ask Yourself:

- What are my expectations for my dog?
- How do I communicate these expectations?
- Am I being realistic, keeping in mind my dog's needs and capabilities?
- Am I, in essence, asking a brown dog to be black? For example, do I expect my shy, fearful dog to enjoy boisterous gatherings of people at our home? Do I expect my anti-social pup to love trips to the dog park?

- And lastly, how much credibility do I have with my dog? When I say "Sit," for instance, does he listen? Or does he look at me knowing I won't follow through on making him obey? Does he call the shots?

Some of you probably have managed to teach your dog some basic commands – sit, stay, stop chewing my Italian-leather loafers. But like many of the owners I work with, I'm guessing you're running into problem areas when it comes to more complicated issues. As with the majority of rocky relationships, a lack of or breakdown in communication is often the culprit. It boils down to learning how to talk to your four-legged friend in a way he understands. Through body language, tone, consistent actions and the right tools, I'm going to teach you to speak Dog. This is a journey into the relationship you share with your dog, not as his "owner" but as his leader. As you improve your communication and strengthen this relationship, you'll begin to build credibility and earn his trust and respect. And yes, you and your dog are "in a relationship," so go ahead and update your Facebook status. As with anyone living under your roof, your dog is part of your family dynamic. He's a thinking, feeling creature with his own way of understanding, communicating and processing. Consider your family – each of you most likely has different communication styles, quirks, preferences, dislikes, ways in which you show love and so on. Your dog is entering this dynamic with his own unique personality, and it's important you know how to effectively communicate to him what you want while simultaneously understanding what he's trying to tell you in various situations. Don't worry – it's not as difficult as it sounds. But until you fully embrace this and learn to speak and understand your dog's language, you two will simply carry on spinning your wheels in counterproductive frustration.

I can't tell you how often owners describe their dogs as unpredictable. "He acts aggressively for no reason," they'll say, exasperated and confused. The truth is, dogs don't do anything "for no reason." Their reactions are instinct driven. The key, as owners, is to understand what motivates them to do what they do and how we contribute to it. Until you tackle him from his level, confusion will continue to arise – especially if it seems as though your dog only listens on his terms. The root of this issue lies in the relationship between you two, and believe you me, he is just as perplexed as you are. He hears you shouting, feels you tugging on the leash, and is fully aware you are upset, but has no idea why. And on the flip side, you hear him bark, feel him lunge, and watch him act aggressively, yet, you are also in the dark. The issue boils down to mixed signals. You think you are clearly communicating your expectations, but chances are, there's lots of room for improvement. You and your dog are speaking two different languages; it's as if you're speaking French and he only understands Italian. Until this communication barrier is broken, exposing the root cause of the issue, your efforts to correct his behavior will get lost in translation. By continuing this cycle, the most you can hope for is treating the symptoms of his behavior, like placing a bucket under a leaky roof. Once we understand each other better, we can then learn ways to change his negative, instinct-driven decisions in a way that makes sense to him. My goal is to provide you with the tools to discover that common language and patch your leaky roof.

All names have been changed to protect the anonymity of the dogs in question.

ABOUT CASSIAN

Born and raised in rural England, I spent countless hours surrounded by animals throughout my childhood. Never having fewer than two dogs at any given time, my parents kept a seemingly open-door policy when it came to pets. I was fascinated and enthralled by our dogs and the relationships we shared with them.

In 1995 I moved to Los Angeles and quickly missed having a dog. After meeting a pit bull named Daisy at a friend's house, I made the decision to find and adopt a dog like her; athletic and powerful but sweet and loving with people. Soon after, I visited my local city shelter and adopted Chief, a pit bull puppy. That trip to the shelter profoundly affected me.

Seeing first-hand the crowded rows of unwanted dogs, I knew I had to help in any way I could. Through volunteering at local rescues and shelters, I suddenly began to realize just how many dogs were surrendered due to behavioral issues. This realization led me to start working with these animals, as well as with trainers, gaining experience helping to train and rehome dogs.

Then, in 2005 Hurricane Katrina hit. Local rescues rallied around this disaster, bringing in dogs from New Orleans who had survived the storm. Working with these dogs as they arrived solidified my passion and drive not only to train dogs, but also to understand them and effectively communicate on a level we both understand. From this, Decoding Dogs was born.

CHAPTER 1

The Roverview

There I stood, my eyes moving between the shaking dog under the bed and the stripper pole firmly mounted in the center of the bedroom.

"He barks at it incessantly. And he's begun peeing on it," the dog's exasperated owner explained. "He's like this with all shiny objects, but the pole really sets him off. I want him to sleep with me, but it's impossible when he spends all night barking and growling." She walked over and gently pried the terrified terrier from his hiding place and nestled him in her arms. I couldn't help but wonder if the dog's issue was rooted in the pole itself, or perhaps something he'd witnessed his owner doing on it. I refrained from asking.

"You see this? What you're doing here? You think you're comforting him, right?" She nodded, kissing Milo on the head. "What you're actually doing is reinforcing his behavior," I continued. "His issue isn't with the pole itself – or any shiny object, for that matter."

"But he's so scared, I just want to make him feel better," she said incredulously.

"He's insecure – that's the root problem. And these behaviors are just symptoms of his insecurity."

"He's not insecure!" she said with a laugh. "He completely runs the show around here!"

"Your lines of communication are out of whack. He's telling you one thing, you're hearing another and you're both reacting accordingly. And wrongly."

Decoding Training

At any given moment, your dog is carrying on a conversation, whether you realize it or not. For some of you, this may be no surprise, as many of us dog people have a tendency to prattle on to our canine companions on a regular basis. But the conversation I'm talking about sometimes is subtler than that. Through body language, actions, reactions, vocalizations and even tone, the two of you are constantly dropping little hints and insights into your personalities, moods, likes, dislikes and expectations of one another. The question is, are these conversations being understood? Are you communicating in a way he understands? Are you able to comprehend what he's saying back? When you come home to find a puddle on your kitchen floor, you probably think, or interrogate loudly, "Why'd you do that?!" And when you then rub his nose in it and banish him to the other room three hours after he's done it, he's wondering, "What'd you do that for?!" In the vast majority of cases, I see that a failure to communicate with and understand one another is the root cause of any issue. And it is your job, as his person, to fix this – to open up the lines of communication and turn your conversations from confusing to constructive. Even though he can't form words, your dog is still trying to tell you things; what makes him happy, what drives him, what stresses him out and what triggers him to react in certain way. I realize this may sound like canine psychobabble, but once you've wrapped your head around this, you'll then have the ability to communicate back to him – which of his behaviors make you smile and laugh and which ones make you wish you'd opted for a goldfish.

The truth is, once you start observing, listening and understanding, you'll find that your dog's not nearly as enigmatic and unpredictable as you might think. You just need a dog decoder ring to help you decipher why he does what he does.

Let's start by lifting the veil of mystery – in many ways, dogs aren't all that different from you and me. They each have individual personalities with particular likes and dislikes. They're social beings who want to know where they stand within their family – am I the leader? A follower? Do I have a job? What are the rules and boundaries? In many ways, they are extremely similar to a two-year-old child; they need and crave structure, routine, stability and consistency. Without it, they will run amuck. And just like with a toddler, you need to be the one to establish boundaries and rules within your family. This sounds logical enough, and while I find most owners understand this concept, they don't know how to implement it. And that's where learning to understand and communicate with your dog comes into play.

In the world of dogs, as it currently stands, there are two extremes I most commonly see among owners. On one hand, there's a strong push to "go to the wild." What this basically means is, dogs descended from wolves, so let's mimic that in our interactions with them. That's why you hear words like Alpha and Pack Leader and hierarchy thrown around so frequently.

On the flip side, you have those who believe dogs are babies; that they should be coddled and snuggled and kept in purses. In my experience, I've come to the conclusion they are neither wolf nor baby – they are a dog-toddler hybrid. Throughout this book, I'll frequently compare dogs to children, but not in the fur baby sense. I don't think they need to be swaddled and cradled and only handled after hand sanitizer is applied. I use the dog-toddler comparison because they are similar when it comes to their need for leadership and guidance. Like kids, dogs need a solid structure and routine, they crave strong but kind leadership, they'll test their boundaries, and as the parent, they look to you for all their needs. But unlike with dogs, you can't drop your kid off at a shelter when you realize you've bitten off more than you can chew or are simply sick of the responsibility.

The second reason I use this comparison is because pretty much everyone can wrap their head around it, even those of you without kids. It helps to bridge the gap and make our dog more relatable, less of an enigma. I think it's easy for us dog owners to become overwhelmed when trying to understand and communicate with our dogs. I mean, they can't speak or understand what we're saying – aside from the word "treat," of course – so this can make expressing our expectations a bit tricky. However, if you sit down and consider how you'd approach this obstacle with a one or two-year-old who can't yet speak, it probably doesn't seem so daunting. As the adult, you set the course. You determine when the child eats, sleeps, plays and so on. You set the boundaries and, little by little, instill them into the child. You determine which behaviors to reward, ignore, or correct. And over time, this slowly teaches him what is acceptable and what isn't, until these expectations are simply a habit. The same goes for raising your dog.

It all boils down to teaching your dog to do what you want him to do and getting him to knock off his shenanigans. I've also come to realize that behavioral issues often reside in smart dogs. This is because the mind of an intelligent dog is always working, moving and searching for stimulation. So congratulations, if you're reading this book, chances are you have a smart dog. However, with great power comes great responsibility – meaning, if you don't provide that mental stimulation, he'll find it on his own. Simply walking your dog for 30 minutes won't wear out his busy little brain – his mind must be exercised, as well.

This book is not designed to merely help you train your dog. My goal is to help you reach your dog on his level and provide you with the tools needed to connect and communicate with him effectively. These methods will gain you your dog's trust and respect, strengthen your relationship, make him see you as a credible and trustworthy leader and ultimately allow you to reclaim your position as head of the house – the Dog Corleone, if you will.

As dog lovers, we have a bad habit of seeing our dogs through rose-tinted glasses when we need to see them in a realistic light. Much like parents who fail to realize how annoying their kids truly can be, we dog owners must acknowledge the truth about our beloved pets. Even if you have the most perfectly mannered dog imaginable, I am confident you can find some tips between these pages that will, at the very least, help you improve that bliss.

Most Common Issues:

- Pulling on the leash
- Barking, lunging and jumping at passersby during walks
- Trepidation or aggression towards new people and/or dogs
- Excessive Barking in the house
- Jumping on people who enter your home.
- Destructive behaviors
- Separation anxiety
- Acting possessively – of you, toys, food, his bed, etc.
- Protectiveness
- Food aggression
- Accidents in the house
- Biting

If you and your dog are suffering from any of those common issues, my bet is, neither of you is happy – at least not in these particular situations. Unless you own a dog for strictly protection purposes, chances are you have a dog purely for the joy of it. However, if you two are constantly at odds, locked in a stressful power struggle during day-to-day activities, I would guess your joie de vivre is currently experiencing a deficit.

What you may not realize is, up to this point, the training techniques you've been using probably only focused on treating the symptoms. You've yet to pinpoint and tackle the root cause. You see, when your dog acts out in any way, this behavior is actually a side effect of a deeper issue. And when you shout or banish him to his crate as punishment, you're only suppressing the effects – not extinguishing the cause. Until you understand *why* he's acting out, the problems will, at best, persist and possibly even worsen.

There is no shortage of techniques, tools, tricks, tips and schools of thought guaranteeing to have your dog so well mannered he'll be fit to dine with kings. From clickers and electric collars to thunder shirts and pills, you can click, shock, clothe and drug your way to a well-behaved dog. So many homes I walk into look like a graveyard for infomercial pet-training products. Maybe I just described your home and the thought of reining in your dog's behavioral issues seems nearly impossible – as if it will take a fleet of experts and a miracle to get a handle on things. It probably seems easier to swipe your credit card and pray for an easy solution or simply stick your head in the sand and accept this as the status quo. Unfortunately, with so many training methods and products out there, it's easy for owners to venture down several paths without any results. There is typically an element of trial-and-error when trying to decode your dog and figure out the most effective way to reach him on his level. Try to learn from your mistakes and experiences. The definition of insanity is repeating the same actions while expecting different results, right? Let's try and avoid this vicious cycle.

For instance, I once worked with a woman who was complaining that her dog had torn apart her trash just a few hours before I'd arrived.

"Has he done that before?" I asked.

"Well, yes," she said. "But I was only gone for 15 minutes."

I paused, calculating in my head how long it would take a dog to knock over a trashcan and go to town. By my estimates, 15 minutes seemed like enough time for that plus a quick nap.

"Was the trashcan empty?" I asked, already knowing the answer simply based on her level of frustration.

"No. I'd just thrown out my leftovers from lunch, so it made a complete mess!"

Learn from your mistakes. This was a dog with a history of dumpster diving, so it's pretty difficult to lay blame on him when you leave a garbage can of goodies right out in the open and then leave him unsupervised for, well, any length of time, really.

Or, if you know your dog gets over-excited when getting attention from new people and has a tendency to jump or become unruly, act accordingly. Ask people to ignore him at first and hold off on affection until he's in a calm, relaxed state of mind. Bottom line, don't repeat what you already know doesn't work. This just compounds frustration and makes the situation all the more overwhelming for all parties involved. As with many of life's challenges, learning how to communicate with, understand and manage your dog actually is not that complicated once you have the right tools and the right information – and can actually be a dog-gone rewarding experience.

Body Language

Recognizing a shift in his stance, a whip of the tail or an elevated ear acts as an early warning system, giving you insight into your dog's current state of mind. Use the following chart to gauge your dog in any given situation. His body will alert you to his mindset and enable you to pick up on things or situations that trigger certain reactions.

CANINE BODY LANGUAGE

Let's Learn the Lingo

- **Dog Trainer** – Dog trainers usually deal with the fundamentals, such as commands, potty training and basic leash work.
- **Dog Behaviorists** – Dog behaviorists delve deeper in search of the causes behind certain behaviors
- **Veterinarians** – Veterinarians deal with physical health and medical issues. While this one may seem pretty obvious, you might be surprised by how many owners seek training and behavior advice from their vets. After all, would you consult a trainer when your dog has a cough or a broken leg?
- **Hierarchy** – By hierarchy, I am referring to a family dynamic. Among wild wolves, this is fairly loose with different members of the pack taking the lead depending on the situation. I do not mean hierarchy as in a rigid, never-changing social structures it's so often used in dog training today.
- **Dominance** – This is a word that gets thrown around a great deal when a dog is acting aggressively, pushy or just being stubborn. However, a truly dominant dog is calm, confident and possesses the ability to read social cues. Other dogs typically gravitate to genuinely dominant dogs, as they are drawn to their calming leadership. Dominance is not the right word in regards to a dog acting aggressively due to insecurity.
- **Submissive** – A submissive dog is the one that calmly rolls on his back, giving you his belly. He is comfortable allowing you to take control. This should not be confused with a dog acting fearful.
- **Pack Leader** – The person who is trusted and respected enough to be in charge, but not simply because he or she says so. This role is earned, like a good boss in an ideal world.
- **Pop/Check** – I use these words interchangeably. A pop or check of the leash is a firm but quick yank on the leash. It's a physical

correction you'll use during the training process. You'll hear me say this numerous times, but here's one more for good measure – this physical correction is always used in conjunction with a verbal command such as, "No" or "Let's go."

- **Reward** – This is pretty self-explanatory, but is commonly misused without you even realizing it. A reward is anything meaningful to your dog that demonstrates your approval. A treat, a pat on the head, rub on the tummy, picking him up, his favorite toy and so on. Anything you give him that he interprets as praise is a reward.
- **Correction** – Correction is a verbal command or physical action you give to discipline unwanted behavior, such as saying "No" or giving a check of the leash.
- **Redirection** – This is a training technique that literally redirects your dog's attention. Perhaps he sees a squirrel, so you lure his attention away with a treat. Or simply turning away from whatever is distracting him is also a form of redirection.
- **Drive** – the instinctual motivating force that compels your dog to act a certain way in given situations. Dogs have three drives; prey, pack and defense.
- **Tone** – I will mention frequently to be aware of your tone of voice. Tone matters. Are you asking or telling? Make sure your tone always lines up with the message you're trying to get across.
- **Credibility** – I will exhaust this word throughout these pages. Credibility is how seriously your dog takes you. How credible are your words and actions? When you give a command, does he listen the first time or wait to see if you'll just give up?
- **Triggers** – Any person, place or thing that elicits a negative reaction from your dog.

Common Training Methods

Just because something's popular, doesn't mean it is necessarily the right route to take. From perms and parachute pants to cars without seatbelts and rubbing whiskey on a teething child's gums, history is riddled with formerly fashionable fads that are now debunked. I'm not saying these training methods are equivalent to liquoring up your kid, but in my experience, they tend to be ineffective and even counterproductive when used alone. popular training techniques circulating through Dogland at the moment.

Pure Positive

The Pure Positive training technique is pretty self-explanatory; it utilizes solely positive feedback to consistently reward a dog's good behavior. While this is a useful way to teach a dog a new command, this method is actually quite unnatural for dogs. Have you ever watched a mother dog with her puppies? Like any mom, she doles out correction when she sees fit. She'll give little nips here and there to keep her kids in line and to teach them which behaviors are acceptable and which are not.

Dogs are wired to understand correction and since the Pure Positive training method eliminates all forms of negative feedback, it lacks a core behavioral modification tool that's so deeply rooted in a dog's wiring. Your dog is already programmed to understand small corrective actions; so doesn't it just make sense to utilize this avenue? To put it into human terms, like us, dogs understand consequences to actions. It's the same as limiting your kid's video game access after they've come home with a lousy report card. It's all about cause and effect. And while it is important to reward good behavior, simply ignoring a bad report card won't keep it from happening again.

Mojo was a boxer I worked with who'd been raised with nothing but pure positive training.

"He's great in the house and on walks in our neighborhood," his dad told me, rubbing Mojo's head. "But when we go to the dog park, it's absolutely impossible to get him to listen. He doesn't come when I call him, he runs away when it's time to go. He's completely unruly."

The reason for this discrepancy in Mojo's behavior is based on the fact that he only really obeys in the house and on walks because he's doing just enough to get that tasty treat or pat on the head. But at the park, his instincts and drive overrule his desire for a reward. The key is to have your dog's trust and respect – like with your children. So that when you say something, they obey not because there might be something in it for them, but because you damn well said so. Without that foundation, your bribes, threats, and shouts are meaningless and you have no credibility. Pure positive training teaches dogs to obey based on a reward, rather than obeying because they respect you and want to do as you say; I call this flying under the radar.

Pack Training

Pack training is a technique that involves bringing a dog into an established group of dogs and relies on them to correct the newcomer's unwanted behavior. The thought behind this method is that a pack of dogs has a social order; with a set of rules and guidelines they'll enforce. If a member of the pack acts out or steps out of line, then the behavior another, higher ranking, dog in the group will correct him. This method also relies on the behavior of the pack to give the trainer the information he needs about the new dog – as opposed to the trainer working with him one-on-one to delve into his issues and personality. This method falls back on the idea of returning to the wild – allowing dogs to function similarly to a wolf pack. Unfortunately, in many cases, the theory behind a dog reconnecting with its wolf instincts isn't very realistic and often sets up the dog and owner for failure upon returning to normal life.

The problem lies in the environment – it typically is not a realistic simulation of the dog's daily life. Unless this technique is executed in an environment very similar to the one the dog will be returning to, this method has a tendency to become less effective on a long-term basis. Think of a criminal sent to prison. While behind bars, he behaves himself; after all, he has Corrections Officers, wardens and even other inmates to keep him in line. To watch him serve his time, an outside observer might think he's changed his ways — turned over a new leaf. However, in many cases, once he is released – free from the watchful eyes of Big Brother – he goes straight back to his old ways.

Dogs are opportunists and if they need to toe the line, they will. But is the dog actually learning new behavior or simply adapting to a different surrounding to ensure his survival? Just like the criminal mentioned above, a dog tends to slip back to his old behaviors once out of the pack training environment. Pack training merely suppresses bad behavior – it doesn't reprogram a dog for the long haul.

Rusty was a mixed bully breed I met in 2015. He'd just completed a 2-week pack training boot camp where he'd won the hearts of all the trainers. When his parents went to pick him up, they were overjoyed to hear how well he'd done and what improvements he'd made.

"He was great for about the first week after we brought him home," his mom told me over the phone. "But then he slowly but surely started acting out again." She sounded exasperated. I went out the following weekend to lend a helping hand. For the first few years of his life, rusty lived chained up in a backyard with little to no human interaction. As a result, he was terrified of everything. And I mean everything. However, rather than cowering and trying to run away, Rusty's fear manifested as fear-based fight drive.

Essentially, something would spook him, like a person passing on the sidewalk, and he'd startle then lunge. Then cower back again. The reason pack training had not solved this was two-fold. First, Rusty was in an unnatural environment that did not mirror his actual life. He became accustomed to pack life but the confidence he acquired during the boot camp quickly receded once he was out of that situation. Secondly, pack training did not equip Rusty's parents with the tools they needed to help him. Rusty was not approached as an individual with his own unique set of issues. And his parents were not informed on how best to manage his fear and insecurities.

In the boot camp, rusty looked to the pack leader for security. However, once that pack leader was removed, he was back in the same place where he'd started. Instead, Rusty's parents needed to know how to establish themselves as his pack leader, how to earn his trust and respect so he could confidently and securely follow their lead. It's not about changing the members of the pack, but rather, altering their roles.

Every dog is different and it's unrealistic to assign one specific training method to any given dog. We understand this about ourselves – everyone is unique. We each have our own way of learning, communicating, accomplishing tasks, comprehending information, reacting in certain situations. Teachers don't walk into classrooms expecting their students to all possess the same learning style. The same goes for dogs. Some are sensitive and insecure, others are dominant and stubborn. Some are naturally dialed into their owners while others may be easily distracted. Because of this, you may find yourself using some trial and error to learn what works best for your dog in different situations. That's to be expected – plus, with each try, you learn more about him.

This is also when it becomes important for you to truly know and understand your dog. To observe his body language and reactions in certain situations, to learn what environments or circumstances trigger fear, insecurity, aggression and confidence. Think of a close friend, spouse or family member – there's a good chance you know what annoys them, delights them, angers them and causes them stress. When you have a tight relationship with someone, you're tuned into them – this is how I want you to become with your dog. Then, as you read this book, you'll begin to understand how you can tailor your communication to his learning style and personality. Is he food motivated? Should you keep treats on hand when working on his training? Is he insecure and needs to build trust in you as his calm but assertive leader? Are you using the most effective tone of voice? Some dogs need very assertive intonations while other may be intimidated by this. What stresses him out? Strangers? Squirrels? A passing skateboard? As you make your way through this book, you will begin to answer these questions and many more.

Common Training Faux Paws

I'm sorry to be the one to tell you, but if your dog has issues, there's a very high chance you're contributing to them in one way or another. And you probably don't even realize it. You know that expression, "The road to Hell is paved with good intentions"? Well, this is often true for the road to an out-of-control canine. When I walk into training sessions, I frequently find myself dumbstruck by the heaps of misinformation owners have been given by so-called experts – friends or family members who happened to have owned a dog or two. If someone has owned three dogs over ten years, all that means is they've only known three dogs…in ten years. Yet, so many who fall under this description love to dole out advice pellets from their dog-training Pez dispenser as if they've seen it all. At best, these nuggets of supposed wisdom are useless. At worst, they can exacerbate existing issues or even create new ones out of thin air. Here are a few of the most common training missteps I run into on a fairly regular basis.

Mistaking Frustration for Assertiveness: We all get frustrated, lose our tempers and raise our voices. When you come home after a long day to find your favorite shoes torn to shreds, it's hard not to lose your cool. But it's important to avoid that energy, tone and body language when correcting your dog. Dogs are very in tune to our emotions and rather than interpreting your yelling as dominance and assertiveness, they see it as weakness. Your dog can see through you and read you like a book. When you're flipping out, he sees it as just that. He needs to respect you and view you as a credible leader — frustration undermines this. True leaders are calm under pressure; they use logic and common sense to resolve problems, not emotional temper tantrums.

Rewarding Fear: Take Milo's mom and the stripper pole for example. Her instinct, upon seeing him freaked out, was to squeeze him tight. Her intentions are great, to comfort her dog when he's afraid. But she's communicating the wrong message to Milo. Because dogs are focused on just one thing at a time, your actions reinforce that thought at that moment. For Milo this means his brain is a'buzzin' with thoughts of fear and insecurity, and when his mom hugs and cuddles him at that moment, she's merely rewarding those thoughts.

Disciplining Fear: On the flip side, disciplining fear is also incredibly ineffective and just downright mean. If your dog's obviously in a fearful state of mind, do you really think shouting at him is the solution? Of course not. Discipline will only serve to further intimidate the dog and perpetuate his fear.

Disciplining After the Fact: I can't tell you how many owners say these words, "I got home from work the other night and he'd peed in the kitchen. So I told him he was a bad dog and put him outside." Let's see here - dogs think in the present, right? They're not looking over their shoulder pondering past mistakes, nor are they peering down the road to analyze potential consequences. You were at work for roughly eight hours. Upon returning, you find a puddle of urine; however, you have no idea how long ago the accident occurred. Maybe five minutes, maybe five hours. Regardless, by you punishing him after the fact, you did nothing but confuse the hell out of him. He doesn't remember doing that. Only discipline in the moment. If you see him squat in the middle of the floor, take action. However, the moment he finishes and walks away, you're too late.

Affection from a Subordinate Position: We all love to give our dogs affection, right? They're so cute and sweet and snuggly. But you need to remember that affection is a form of communication to your dog. If your dog respects you, obeys your commands and treats you as the leader of the family, then showing him affection is fine. However, if you've yet to earn his respect, give affection sparingly. Don't confuse respect with liking you. A dog can trust you without respecting you. I don't care how much he follows you around the house and crawls into your lap. If he doesn't sit when you tell him or he continuously tests his boundaries with you, then you ain't got his respect. But don't worry, we're going to fix that. And in the meantime, only love on him after he's earned it.

Affection at the Wrong Time: Again, dogs only think about one thing at a time and affection communicates a message to them. Therefore, if your dog's busy little brain is up to no good, don't give him a love squeeze. You'll see owners do this all the time. We've probably all done it, in fact. Your dog's fixating on a squirrel or barking its head off, so you crouch down and rub his neck or give him a pat on the head. No! All that does is reinforce those cheeky thoughts swirling around his mind.

Justifying: Avoid justifying your dog's bad behavior. "Oh, he's small so his aggression isn't hurting anyone." Sure it is — it's hurting him. Maybe not physically, but it's coming from a place of fear or anxiety or insecurity and needs to be fixed. I worked with a guy named Joey and his Chihuahua/ Pomeranian mix, Boo. Joey called me because Boo had been showing signs of possessiveness that were becoming hard to manage.

"He humps my arm. Like, all the time," Joey said when I arrived.

"What do you mean?" I asked, wondering how Joey was allowing this tiny dog to go at it on his arm.

"At night when I'm watching television, he hops up on the couch and humps my arm incessantly."

"How long has this been going on?" I asked.

"Pretty much since I got him nearly a year ago."

"A year?!"

"Well, I figured it was good exercise for him."

This is a prime example of an owner justifying a behavior that's rooted in something deeper. Because Joey had it in his mind that Boo's humping was providing him a decent cardio workout, he simply justified the symptom. Leaving the root cause unresolved. If your dog is acting badly, don't defend or justify. Accept and remedy.

Allowing Your Dog to Control the Environment: I recently worked with a couple whose dog had been acting most strangely. So much so, they even took her into the vet before our session because they were convinced she was sick. She wasn't walking or eating – except for when her parents made her scrambled eggs. Then she'd eat. They literally carried her from room to room on a pillow, absolutely sure she was terribly ill. After receiving a clean bill of health, I helped them realize the diagnosis was nothing more than manipulation. Obviously, if you think your dog may be sick, go to the vet. But the minute health issues are ruled out, it's time to realize the problems are behavioral.

Unrealistic Expectations: I am constantly astounded by the unrealistic expectations people set for their dogs. "Please train my dog to poop in the southwest corner of my yard," an owner once told me, as if I'm a wizard capable of mind control. "He barks," an owner will say, demonstrating how their dog gives one or two quick barks any time the doorbell rings. He's a dog! Make sure your expectations are reasonable, for both dogs in general and yours in particular.

On the other hand, there are times I walk in and find myself blown away by what an owner will tolerate. Destroyed shoes, stuffing falling out of furniture, bite and claw marks on their arms. In this case, the expectations are too low and need to be raised a notch or two. Don't just accept total chaos and havoc, but also know that dogs are dogs – and if that's unacceptable to you, get a fish next time.

Effective Training Techniques

Correction and redirection are the two main techniques used to change, discipline, and reinforce behaviors in dogs. These two methods can be used both individually and in tandem, depending on the situation and what message you're trying to send. You will first want to establish what drive your dog is currently in, what instinct is motivating him at that moment. Don't worry if this doesn't make sense right now – by the end of Chapter 4, you'll be a drive-detecting genius. Next, when it comes to correcting or redirecting your dog, timing is key; you want to correct and/or redirect your dog before he even has a chance to act. Watch his body language, know his triggers, and launch a preemptive strike. If you wait until after he's acted, the situation could become sticky, leaving you with no option other than damage control.

Correction is essentially punishment, to put it into human terms. Correcting a dog's unwanted behavior involves doling out a consequence for whatever it is he just did. Correction is a reaction to his action – teaching him, for example, that when he barks excessively, he'll then get spritzed in the face with a spray bottle. Or, when he tenses up or frowns at the sight of another dog on walks, he'll then receive a pop with the leash. Let me reiterate, because it's so important – correct your dog's thoughts, don't wait until he's lunged into action. Correction is both physical and verbal. As you physically correct him, also do so verbally – "No!" or "Leave it!" And remember, tone matters. Are you telling him to leave it in an assertive voice or asking him passively? The combination of verbal and physical builds his association between the two – after time, you should be able to simply correct him verbally, phasing out the physical.

Spray bottles and leashes are the two best tools for physical correction. I advise using the spray bottle not only in your house, but even taking it with you on walks if your dog is especially problematic in that setting. But always use these in tandem with verbal correction, as this helps your dog to better understand your expectations and form a negative association to that specific unwanted behavior. After a while, it will become crystal clear to him that certain behaviors result in negative consequences, causing him to cut them out in order to avoid those consequences.

Redirection, on the other hand, is a system reboot, so to speak. This method uses your dog's recall abilities – the Come command – to redirect his attention from whatever it is that's stressing him out and refocusing back onto you. Treats come in very handy when trying to regain your dog's focus. Redirection is most effectively used before your dog reacts to the trigger – shift his thoughts before he has an opportunity to misbehave. When you see his body language change or you spot a potential trigger ahead, use the Come command and recall him back to you. Give him a treat and get him dialed in – perhaps put him in a Down-Stay, get him to make eye contact, or simply turn and walk the other way.

Correction and redirection can also be used together. For instance, if you're walking down the street and your dog sees a squirrel, the moment you notice him become distracted, overly-stimulated and excited, or even aggressive, you can give him a pop with the leash, say "No!" and then redirect him back to you. Be mindful of your tone and body language. If you're correcting, assert yourself in both. However, if you want to redirect him back to you, a forceful "Come!" from a standing posture could send the wrong message. In this case, crouch down and make your body and tone welcoming. There may be some trial and error as you figure out which methods works most efficiently on your dog, as they are all different. Some pups need that physical correction to snap them out of it, while others are more easily bribed through redirection and a tasty treat. Then there are those auditory dogs that prove very responsive to verbal communication. I find using correction and redirection in tandem the best method, as it's always helpful to give your dog something else to focus on after correcting him – an alternative distraction, if you will.

As we know, dogs are very routine-oriented. Most of their habitual behaviors have gradually formed and even gotten worse over time. Because of this, It's important to set realistic expectations – you may not be able to solve these issues with the first pop of the leash and an assertive verbal correction. Know your dog's threshold – if he's aggressive towards other dogs once they're within fifty feet, work with him at that distance, don't push it until he's made progress. By correcting and redirecting him within his natural threshold, you can give him a longer fuse – after some work, you'll find he maintains his composure until the other dog is within thirty feet, then twenty, and so on. The ultimate goal is to decrease his reaction to triggers by doing less and less as you go. As his association to those triggers changes and his fuse lengthens, the methods you use to correct and redirect him should lessen; meaning, if in the beginning you use verbal and physical correction along with redirection, as you go along, you should be able to wean him off the physical correction, then maybe any correction at all, until you're left with just a simple redirecting "Come." Start with what works then go from there.

Common Training Tools

Each session I go on I take with me my handy bag of training gear. In it is a smorgasbord of collars, harnesses, leashes and spray bottles. The reason I lug this around with me is, not all dogs are the same. Thus, no one particular collar or corrective method is going to work effectively on all dogs. Proper training equipment boils down to the right tool used on the right dog in the right way. I'm not here to tell you which one is best for your dog. I just want to give you a run-down of what's out there and a general idea of which tool typically works best for certain situations. I leave it to you, however, to trial and error your way into fitting your dog with the most appropriate gear for his needs. Do your research, educate yourself and don't lose hope if you don't strike gold the first time. Just ask about return and refund policies so you don't end up having to take out a second mortgage in the process.

Retractable Leash: Also known as a flexi-leash. This tool is appropriate…never. Seriously. Never. Ever. They provide you with zero control, allow your dog to run around like a wild banshee and they're unsafe. How, you may ask? Leash burn, for starters. With 15-20 feet of slack, that thin cord is just waiting to wrap around you or your dog's leg and leave its blistering mark. Also, with that much leash and just a handle to control it, reeling your dog back in can prove challenging – which isn't exactly ideal when he bolts out into the middle of the street. Just trust me. If you have a flexi-leash, trash it, burn it, bury it. It's not giving your dog freedom. It's giving him 20 feet of rope with which to get into trouble.

No-Slip/Martingale Collar: Martingales are a good starting point when beginning your training tool search. These collars provide slightly more control than your normal buckle or easy-release collar. They slip over the head and are designed to tighten as your dog pulls against you. They typically aren't enough for your body-builder breeds whose strength and tenacity rival those of a bull. But for a dog that responds quickly and easily to slight correction and only pulls a little on the leash, this collar provides an extra layer of control. But don't keep it constantly cinched. The tightening function should be used as a correction. If your dog pulls or lunges, give the leash a quick but firm check (pull), along with a verbal command (i.e. No, leave it or let's go). The goal is to correct behavior, not choke out your dog.

Prong Collar: Prongs are those spiky collars that to the untrained eye, more resemble a torture device than a dog training tool. Well, I'm here to bust that myth – prongs are not evil nor does using one constitute animal cruelty. If used improperly, however, then yes, they're not very nice. When I see one on a three-pound Chihuahua, I question that owner's sensibility. Or when I watch someone walk their dog down the sidewalk with the prong permanently dug into the poor fella's neck, I have to fight the urge to pry the leash out of their hand. With that said, here's a secret – I use prongs on both my dogs. I've had and worked with many strong, stubborn pits who like to test their boundaries on walks. The prongs allowed me to correct their shenanigans until the time came when I felt confident their training had sunk in and we graduated up to Martingales. These collars are strictly corrective. They are not to be used like a harness, to keep your dog from pulling. They're best suited for large, strong dogs who need correction. When you're not giving a corrective check, the leash should maintain slack and the prong shouldn't be tight. Like with the no-slip collar, always use the physical correction – the check of the leash – in conjunction with a verbal command. The end goal is to get your dog to respond to the verbal command alone. Just an FYI – prongs should not be used on dogs with neck issues. Also, I've encountered numerous dogs who have bad associations to prong collars – usually because they've been used to excess. In these cases, the prong can actually trigger stress and anxiety-induced meltdowns. Meaning, the training tool is actually working against you. Take the path of least resistance if you find yourself in this position and choose a different collar. Lastly, be sure to buy a high-quality prong, as some sold at common pet stores can be too sharp. Look for one with rounded prongs rather than pointy ones.

Halti/Gentle Leader: I'm sure you've seen these. A Halti is a collar that wraps around the dog's muzzle rather than his neck. Though they can be a bit awkward to get used to – for both you and your dog – they're really quite effective for dogs that are extremely visual. By giving you control of the dog's head, you can physically redirect his attention away from triggers or distractions. I also like them for dogs that have bad associations with being corrected around the neck. In cases where overcorrection has occurred and a dog is actually triggered by a prong or no-slip collar, a Halti is a great alternative. And if your dog is a bit nippy on the leash, maybe consider this tool. It gives you control of their muzzle and even provides somewhat limited mobility in that area. I tend to prefer Haltis over Gentle Leaders due to the safety clip feature that helps prevent your dog from slipping out and getting off-leash.

Harness: I don't typically recommend harnesses, as they give you little control or ability to correct or redirect your dog. Plus, pulling against a harness can actually be enjoyable for the dog. It makes him work harder to get that cat or squirrel, builds his excitement and gives no corrective consequence. Not to mention, it doesn't help that it sits right around the strongest part of your dog. However, if your dog is perfectly happy on the leash and just trots along by your side, a harness is a fine option. They're also a good alternative for dogs with neck issues. Just make sure you get one that fits properly – you don't want your dog finagling his way out of it and streaking through the neighborhood naked.

Electronic Collar: This training tool is used as a replacement for verbal commands; I frequently implement it when working with deaf dogs. Also known as a remote training collar or a shock collar, this sucker is an effective tool when used properly. However, on the flip side, it can exacerbate issues, create new ones and just be downright cruel when administered the wrong way. A good aspect of this collar is that you can tailor the level of correction to the extent to which your dog is misbehaving. Before even turning the collar on, take your dog for a walk with it around his neck. Let him get used to it and create positive associations with it before you start doling out shocks. The goal of an electronic collar is to make your dog believe his negative behavior is directly causing the consequence – the shock. You and the collar have nothing to do with it. Always start at the lowest level and gauge your dog's response. Maybe his ear twitches or he moves his head, as if to get away from the collar. If he doesn't react, slowly turn the transmitter to the next level and try again. Always, always, always use this collar in conjunction with a verbal command. Electronic collars aren't meant to be used on a permanent basis. Your end game is to use the physical consequence as a way to instill the verbal commands into your dog's little head until you can take the correction out of the picture altogether. If you go this route, do your research. Talk to someone who knows what they're doing and always stay mindful of how you're using it. You're wanting to correct bad habits, not singe his whiskers off. Like with the prong, be sure to buy high-quality.

Muzzle: Muzzles are a tricky tool. Like with many of these tools, you first need to make sure you're using the right one. Please don't buy one that impedes your dog's mouth mobility, usually called a mesh muzzle. I strongly advise buying a basket muzzle; it goes around your dog's snout, but he can still sniff, pants and move his mouth. It looks a bit like the apparatus worn by Hannibal Lecter, but it creates a solid barrier between your dog's mouth and a potential victim of nipping. Muzzles should be used mainly as a safety precaution. If you know your dog is a bit of a biter but you have to walk him in an area where people or other dogs are unavoidable, a muzzle is a good option. But don't decide you're going to take your dog-aggressive pup to the park and use a muzzle to prevent any incidents. If he's biting at people or other dogs, there's a reason, so avoid those situations whenever possible. And for the times human or dog interaction can't be prevented, his Hannibal Lecter mask will keep everyone safe.

Spray Bottle: This is one of my favorite training tools. Most people have them lying around in a cupboard somewhere, but if you don't, you can get one for about a dollar. Take your normal, run-of-the-mill spray bottle (preferably not one that previously contained a hazardous chemical), fill it up with water and you're good to go. You can use this tool on walks, in the backyard and inside your home. When your dog acts out, just give him a couple spritzes and watch him recoil. Always combine this tool with a verbal correction – he needs to respect you as the bearer of the spray bottle. When this tool works, it really works; usually getting to a point where all you have to do is reach for the bottle and he'll respond accordingly. I have run across dogs who enjoy getting sprayed or try to lick the water as it's coming at them. If yours is like this, obviously this is not an effective option for you. But because it's so inexpensive and easily accessible, there's no harm in giving it a shot – I mean, spray.

I'm a big promoter of the path of least resistance, meaning, start with the simplest tool and work your way up from there. If a 69-cent spray bottle does the trick, great. There's no reason to cause yourself or your dog extra frustration by trying to use a complicated, potentially uncomfortable and pricy product if it's not necessary. Make life as easy as possible for the both of you. Don't get sucked in by late-night infomercials or the teenage cashier at your local pet store and take home something you simply don't need. Just find the right tool for your dog and use it the right way.

If you do find that one of the more elaborate tools is best – like a prong or e-collar – just know that you can graduate up later once the training has really taken hold. As I said, I used to use prongs on my dogs, but now they just wear Martingales. You should aim to reach the point where the simplest tool works for you. Another interesting note, it's not uncommon for dogs to form an association to a certain tool. I once worked with a dog who had been trained with a bark collar, but his association was so strong, just slipping it over his neck without even turning it on did the trick.

CHAPTER 2

Let's Get Philosophical

Decoding the Philosophy

I watched as Isabel made her way down the sidewalk, swapping leashes from hand-to-hand, hopscotching over dogs as they darted this way and that and yanking and tugging as each of her four pups lunged in different directions. It was quite a scene. Heads turned, but probably not for the reason she'd have liked. As I called her and the gang of "terrierists" back to me, I couldn't help but wonder how she dealt with this mayhem.

"They're just a feisty foursome," she said as her gang began circling around her, calf-roping her legs with their leashes. She looked down, "I guess I'm just used to it. Plus, they're really well behaved inside, so there's that." I found that hard to believe. And even more so a few moments later when a woman and her child passed by on the sidewalk. I watched as one dog stood next to her, relaxed but vigilant. Another slunk to the ground and attempted to army crawl between Isabel's legs. The third, and tiniest I might add, lunged and barked with all her might while the fourth simply spun in circles yapping his head off.

"Really?" I asked incredulously. "They're good inside?" She laughed and nodded. I helped her extricate herself from the web of leashes wrapped around her calves and we headed into her apartment. And wouldn't you know it, things were not quite as peachy indoors as Isabel thought. I mean, they were fine inside, but they were really just flying under the radar. What this means is, Isabel didn't have many rules for them inside, as they were little and pretty easy. So there was rarely a time when she challenged them to obey her indoors. Because of this, Isabel was never forced to work on obedience in her apartment, so once she stepped out her front door, she had no training foundation to fall back on when they got unruly. The barking, lunging, and refusal to listen or obey were not the actual issues but merely symptoms. If I'd simply instructed Isabel to carry a spray bottle on her walks and give them a spritz whenever they acted up, this would just be a surface-deep remedy. A Band-Aid effect. It might quell their howls and distract them for a hot minute, but it wouldn't solve the issue at hand. By delving more deeply and getting to the root of the problem, we can fix it at its source.

You see, Isabel is legally blind. And while she's perfectly capable and independent, there had been times when dogs or people blindsided her, literally. She'd be walking along then all a sudden, she'd look up and someone would be right next to her, in front of her or passing by her. Naturally, this gave her a startle – especially at night. I began to realize her dogs were picking up on this via her energy. It wasn't that they were perfectly behaved inside, it was simply a case of no triggers. Once outdoors, they felt she was no longer in charge. This caused each of them to react in different ways depending on each one's individual personality, triggers, drive and role in the family.

Once we discovered the root cause – Isabel's dogs losing trust and credibility in her leadership abilities outside — I was able to show Isabel effective ways to tackle the issues on each dog's level. Obviously having four dogs meant more moving parts, more dogs to understand, observe and communicate to, and more opportunities for chaos. But once she understood where each was coming from and why they reacted as they did, she was able to modify the attitude and approach she used in any given situation according to each dog's needs. If I'd just sent her off with a spray bottle and a handshake, she'd probably be in the hospital with third-degree leash burn by this point.

I don't buy into the idea that it's as simple as just proclaiming oneself the pack leader, treating your dogs like wolves and coming at them from a dominant position. They are members of our family. When your child acts out, I assume you don't pin him on his back as a show of dominance. Or if your significant other doesn't take out the trash after you've asked five times, I doubt you loom over him as a reminder of who's the Alpha. Rather, you approach each of these situations with understanding and communication. Through trial-and-error and experience, you've learned how to get the most out of the people around you. For example, maybe you've figured out that lecturing your child does no good, but putting him in time out for ten minutes snaps him back into line. So that has become your go-to approach. And with your significant other, maybe you've figured out that nagging gets you nowhere, but sweetly asking as you hand him his favorite snack gets that trash taken out immediately. My point is, through experience, you've learned how to approach various people in your life on their terms, in a way they respond to and understand. In fact, you probably don't even have to think about it anymore, these approaches have just become habits over time. And this brings me to the crux of my philosophy regarding dog training.

The SHARK Effect

All through school, I used acronyms as a study technique; a way to parse information in a way I could understand and retain. So, it only makes sense that I'd do the same when laying out my dog training philosophy. The SHARK Effect centers around easy, manageable steps you can take day-by-day. Individually, these steps may seem small, but over time they build on each other and take root in your daily life. Let me break it down for you.

Simple: I'm all about the path of least resistance. Find what works for you and makes your life easier. Start slow, taking gradual steps towards change. With Isabel, I had her split her walks into two. Rather than one 30-minute rollercoaster of canine chaos, she took two dogs at a time for fifteen minutes. This was a simple step that made her life easier. She could give each dog more attention and work with him on his terms as situations arose.

Habits: As you implement these simple changes they'll start to become part of your daily life. Before you know it, they're a habit. You won't even have to stop and think about it, like brushing your teeth. It's simply part of your routine. I instructed Isabel to walk her most secure dog with the one who exhibited the most fear. She sent me a text two weeks later telling me that for the first few days, it was tough. She kept forgetting who went with whom. But by the two-week mark, not only did she not have to think about it, even the dogs knew who went outside on which shift. It became a habit for everyone involved.

Affecting: As these simple modifications take root in your daily life they'll gradually begin to compound and create a ripple effect. In that same update text, Isabel told me she was starting to see positive changes in each of her dogs. While her walks weren't perfect yet, they were becoming more enjoyable and less of an insanity-inducing experience.

Results: When Isabel first came to me, her hope and goal was to get her dogs to stop acting like a pack of wild hyenas on their walks. However, by taking focus off the symptoms, learning the root cause and taking small steps to tackle the underlying issues, she was not only able to achieve her goal, but also gain real results. Rather than just suppressing the obvious, surface-level issues – the barking, lunging and ducking for cover – she was actually able to alter her dogs' associations and find ways to effectively communicate to them in a way they each understood. Their behaviors changed, but not because of a shock collar, spray bottle or magic word. Through the simple alterations she made to her approach, Isabel was able to gain the trust of each of her dogs which created a shift in how they reacted.

Knowledge: As you implement this philosophy into your dog training, you'll find yourself gaining new insights into your dog and yourself. You'll become more observant, better understand why he does what he does and possess the tools and deep knowledge to head off any issues at the pass. Like in Isabel's case, once she cracked the code and fully understood why her dogs were acting as they were and the role she played in it, she was able to use her knowledge to gain credibility with them. She translated what she'd learned into effective and sustainable tools. Training is an ongoing process with a dog. Once you've gotten him to a point where you're happy, that's when management comes in. It's then time to maintain those results. But just like with us, dogs can change over time. Old triggers may fade away as new ones pop to the surface. But you'll be prepared. You'll have a deeper understanding of where he's coming from and why he's reacting in a certain way. And you'll know how to approach it. Like with your husband and that pesky trash he refuses to take out, you simply just know how to handle it.

Isabel's case was interesting, and seemingly very difficult, because of all the moving parts. Four dogs, a visual impairment and numerous varying reactions in any given situation. The key was to take it piece by piece, step by step. Like with any daunting obstacles, if you try to tackle it in its entirety, it can become overwhelming. But once you start slowly chipping away, one layer at a time, you find it's not nearly as scary or impossible as you thought.

CHAPTER 3

Can You Relate?

It is true in any relationship, finding common ground is important, and satisfying. It helps you relate to one another, understand each other and opens up lines of communication. This is especially true in a relationship that's making its way through choppy waters. If you can't relate, then it's difficult to understand the other party's point of view and perspective. This then makes communication all the more challenging. With many of my clients, I find myself wearing several hats: dog trainer, human trainer, family therapist and interpreter.

"I just want him to love me," Michael said, looking across the room at his hound mix. "But he doesn't seem to give a damn about me."

It was a tale as old as time, that of unrequited love. At least that was Michael's take on the situation.

"Why don't you think he loves you?" I asked, knowing his response would tell me pretty much everything I needed to know.

"He doesn't want to snuggle with me, he doesn't follow me around. And he never gives me kisses."

"Right," I said, trying to find a way to let Michael down easy. "I fear you may have unrealistic expectations here, and you're burdening Buddy here with your own emotional needs. He's his own dog with his own set of needs."

"But I want a dog that is affectionate."

"Hounds are working dogs," I told him. "They tend to be more aloof, extremely smell oriented which keeps them constantly alert and they typically want to earn their keep. They aren't generally real big on affection."

Michael couldn't wrap his head around this

"You may have a case of irreconcilable differences," I said as nicely as possible. What I really wanted to tell Michael was, "That's what your wife is for," but I didn't have it in me.

Different Strokes

Buddy and Michael are a prime example of an inability to relate to one another. They're each seeking very different needs from their relationship and they're both losing. Michael chose Buddy because he loves the look of hounds; their floppy ears, soulful eyes and long kissable noses. Appearance, in any relationship, is only skin deep, as they say. Rather than choosing a dog based on emotional connection and temperament, he made his decision off of attributes that in no way guarantee a successful relationship.

As I've said repeatedly, knowing your dog and understanding what makes him tick are the key to a healthy relationship. However, knowing him isn't enough. You also need to accept him for who he is, warts and all. I think most people would agree this is true for our relationships with one another, as well. You can't jump into a marriage expecting to overhaul your spouse's entire personality. Sure, you can probably make tweaks here and there if you have the right approach, but at the end of the day, he is who he is. I'm also pretty sure compromise comes into play from time to time, proving fairly helpful as we navigate the waters of our various relationships. You'll find that acceptance and compromise are useful tools in the relationship you have with your dog, as well.

Let's look back at Michael for a minute. Buddy likes to work, feel useful and earn his keep, so to speak. Michael wants affection. So what's the solution? First Michael had to accept Buddy for Buddy. He's not a dog that's going to curl up on the couch and nuzzle into his owner. However, with the right approach, it was possible to make Buddy more receptive. Michael's next step was to compromise. He'd put Buddy to work through training. Then, after Buddy sat, stayed and came, he'd be more responsive and welcoming to Michael's snuggles and kisses. Not only did the training work Buddy's mind, which was something he craved, it also made him more obedient and strengthened his relationship with Michael through trust and respect. Once Michael modified his approach based on Buddy's needs, he was better able to relate to him and in turn, communicate with him.

One of the more common complaints I hear from owners is that their dog isn't friendly towards people or other dogs. Maybe he barks and lunges or cowers under your feet in fear. Owners have a tendency to put their own likes and dislikes onto their dogs. I like sitting outside at cafes, so my dog should, too. Meanwhile, your poor pup is shaking under the table, flinching every time someone walks by.

Let's step into his paws for a moment. When you go to the grocery store, or pop to the post office to mail a package, or simply walk down the street, do you want to be approached by everyone you encounter? For some of you, the answer may be, "Sure! I love meeting new people." But for others, the idea of interacting with complete strangers while you're merely trying to pick out the ripest peach sounds like a nightmare. Dogs are the same. In the sense that they're each completely different. Some dogs are extroverts and enjoy socializing and meeting anyone willing to give a second look their way. Others simply can't be bothered to even give you the time of day. And for some, it causes stress, fear or excessive stimulation. For them, it boils down to trust. Certain dogs have trust issues and insecurities, making new environments, situations, and people potentially very unpleasant. I'm guessing you don't expect one of your friends to like everything you do, so don't expect this from your dog. If you like sitting outside on patios but he'd prefer being at home, call an equally social human friend and leave your dog be. Just like us, a dog can have social anxiety, as well. That doesn't mean he needs a team of therapists. It just means he doesn't like being groped by strangers, it causes stress. I mean, buy him a drink first.

Unlike your friends, your dog can't open his mouth and flat out tell you he hates being around groups of people. He's going to communicate this to you in the only way he knows how — be it growling, cowering or even nipping And let me tell you, tact and social grace are probably not his strong suit. Where as you might nicely smile, nod your head and turn away in order to stop an unwanted interaction, your dog is more likely to show a bit less courtesy. If a situation is making your dog uncomfortable, he'll give subtle indications at first. Often times, however, due to our lack of understanding, these early warning signs go unnoticed, leaving the dog to resort to more vehement measures.

Another issue I see is owners projecting their emotions onto their dog. Like with Michael. He wanted to dole out affection and expected Buddy to eagerly welcome it. Or maybe you're feeling sad and turn to your dog for consolation, only to find him entrenched in play mode. For some owners this causes frustration, confusion and even hurt feelings. We need to learn that our dogs are not at our beck-and-call, constantly available to gel to our exact mood and whim. These are behaviors within ourselves that we need to avoid. I recently worked with a dog named Charlie whose owner regularly took him with her to coffee shops, cafes, and outdoor restaurants. But Charlie hated these outings – they caused him stress and anxiety, which led to him misbehaving in these settings. When I asked his owner why she continued to take him, she said, "I don't want him to feel that he's missing out." I tried to assure her Charlie was not suffering from a fear of missing out. That feeling of being excluded is unique to humans. Sure, he might act like he wants to tag along as you head for the front door, but rest assured that within five minutes of you leaving, he's happily doing his own thing. In the case of Charlie, he'd actually be much happier left at home to relax with a tasty bone.

To your dog, every approaching person is equal to a conversation in our world. And different dogs will respond in different ways. So it's important to understand how yours takes to these types of situations. In cases when an interaction is necessary – say, you have guests over – watch what your dog is saying as the new people approach. Like us, dogs give subtle signals when they're uncomfortable. Where you might twirl your hair, shift from foot to foot, or laugh awkwardly, they also exhibit certain changes in their personality, posture or mannerisms. Dogs will turn to a behavior known as Practicing Avoidance, where he tucks his tail, avoids eye contact, shrinks back towards his owner in an attempt to get under or on top of their feet or will lean against them. The dog's body language will indicate his overall attempt to make himself appear small and not engage or interact.

Like us, dogs will override the physical in favor of the emotional – meaning, if your dog is scared during a walk, he may lunge as an emotional response, despite the fact this might cause him pain. As humans we constantly do this; we smoke, drink, and eat fatty, greasy food despite the physical effects. Why? Because we receive an emotional release by doing so. Our bodies tell us otherwise, just like a collar pinching into a dog's neck, but our emotions are speaking more loudly. This often baffles owners. "He lunges so hard he chokes and coughs. It's bizarre!" Not really. Something is triggering him to a point the consequences be damned, this is worth it. Think of your last bad breakup. How'd you cope? A night of drinking with your buddies? Dancing and drinks with your girlfriends? Maybe a bad haircut? Chances are, your reaction probably wasn't healthy and most likely made you feel like hell the next day. But in that moment, despite knowing the consequences, you decided it was all worth it. Surely you can relate.

For those of you out there finding it difficult to relate to your dog's personality, find hope through Michael and Buddy. Luckily, acceptance and compromise tend to be far easier with a dog than a human. Think outside the box and find ways for you two to connect and each gain something out of any given situation. Once you guys get on the same page and find some common ground, you'll be well on your way to getting the most out of each other. Look at him as you would a significant other. Your dog is who he is and though he may not be perfect, there are ways to get things back on track. And at least with your dog, you don't have to deal with his overbearing mother.

CHAPTER 4

What Makes Your Dog Tick?

As I walked into the house, Sparkles the Great Dane was happily chewing on a toy. From the other room I could hear her going to town on the squeaker.

"She's fine because you didn't ring the doorbell or knock," her mom said after greeting me on their front porch.

"Then let's see, shall we?" I said, walking back outside alone. The moment I rang the doorbell I heard the frenzy commence. Sparkles came rushing at the door, barking with all her might, which is pretty darn intimidating, as you can imagine. Her mom let me in, attempting to calm her small horse. After a few seconds Sparkles came trotting up to me, wagging her tail and greeting me with the same gusto as when she was in attack mode. The three of us walked into their living room and after a few more nudges for attention, Sparkles went back to her toy.

In this 3-minute timeframe, Sparkles demonstrated all three Drives – the instinctual motivators that compel our dogs to behave a certain way in a particular situation. It's their "why," their instinctive driving force. Sparkles went from Prey to Defensive to Pack and then back to Prey in that one flash of activity. My mission was to teach Sparkles' mom how to control the situation and switch her from one drive to another as needed.

Remember in the Introduction when I said dogs don't do anything for no reason? They always have a *why* – something that's driving them to do what they do. Like people, the actions of your dog are motivated by something. Let's take you, for example. What drives you? What triggers you to respond the way you do in any given situation? If you're provoked, do you hit back or run for the hills? Are you motivated by praise and accolades? It may be hard to pinpoint exactly why you react the way you do. But chances are, you have a fairly good idea of how you'll react.

Understanding what drives your dog and learning which situations will elicit which reactions is such a helpful tool in combating behavioral issues. Not only is it yet more insight into who your dog is, but through your powers of observation and past experience with your dog, you may actually be able to stop your dog in his tracks before he misbehaves.

There are three primary drives that influence a dog's behavior in any given situation. Understanding what drives your dog will give you insight into his unique little personality and why he's more difficult in certain situations than others. Maybe you have a close friend who gets road rage, so you avoid rush-hour car trips with her. Or maybe you know your spouse gets cranky if they haven't eaten, so you save your nagging or criticism for after dinner. And chances are, you've learned these pieces of information through past experience. The same is true with your dog. As I've said, he's not nearly as enigmatic as you think. In fact, his behaviors are downright predictable based on how he's acted in the past in similar situations. It all boils down to understanding what's buzzing around in his busy little brain at any given moment.

Chances are, you already know and understand more than you think. Do you tense up at the sight of an oncoming bicycle, jogger or baby stroller? If so, this is because you already know what's about to happen – and it ain't good.

Prey Drive:

Prey Drive is commonly seen on the leash. It's the instinct that kicks in when your dog sees a cat or squirrel. Molly, a 3-year-old hound mix I trained, had as strong a prey drive as it gets. One minute she'd be moseying along next to her dad and then a split second later she'd be in full Prey Drive. Between her sight and smell, it didn't take much to flip this switch.

Behaviors Associated with Prey Drive Include:

- Seeing, hearing and smelling
- Air scenting and tracking
- Stalking and chasing
- Pouncing
- High-pitched barking
- Jumping up and pulling down
- Shaking an object
- Tearing and ripping apart
- Biting and killing
- Carrying
- Eating
- Digging and burying
- Lunging on the leash

Prey Drive is a behavior associated with our dog's instinct to kill, chase and eat. It is triggered through motion, sound and smell. Watch how your dog reacts the next time he sees a squirrel run up a tree. If he gives it a look then returns to what he was doing, he's not strong in Prey Drive. However, if he lunges, barks or jumps, you've got a hardened predator on your hands, even if he is in the body of a Maltipoo.

Pack Drive:

Pack Drive is as it sounds – the dog is driven by instinct to be part of his pack.

I stood in the kitchen as three dogs circled around me, tails wagging and noses covering every inch of my shoes and pants.

"They're a happy family," their mom said, looking down at her Chihuahua, beagle and pit/mastiff mix. "I worry about Roxy, the Beagle, running away when we go to the park, though."

I looked down at the trio. Being so smell-oriented, Roxy was definitely a bit of an off-leash risk.

"She never comes when I call her. She's always just so distracted."

"How have you not lost her yet?" I asked.

"I just start playing with the other two and she comes running over. When I yell her name, begging her to come and bribing her with treats, she totally ignores me. But the minute I start playing around with the other two or the pack starts moving, she's there in a flash."

"That's her Pack Drive kicking in," I said. "You're lucky it's so strong."

Behaviors Associated with Pack Drive Include:

- Physical contact with people and/or other dogs
- Playing with people and/or other dogs
- Behaviors associated with social interaction with people and other dogs, such as reading body language
- Reproductive behaviors, such as licking, mounting, washing ears, and all courting gestures
- Following the leader
- The ability to breed and to be a good parent

Dogs high in Pack Drive tend to be your more sociable animals. They exhibit behaviors associated with reproduction – like grooming and licking. They enjoy playing with other dogs or people and are comfortable living within a group. A dog with strong Pack Drive tends to toe the line and follow rules, as well. He's very responsive to praise through touch. These gestures are extremely meaningful to him and get his attention. Pack Drive is an instinct inherited from wolves, but in our modern-day dogs, it translates as a willingness to live as part of a human group and a willingness to work with us as a teammate.

Defense Drive:

Defense Drive manifests in two ways – fight and flight. Rufus was a big old mastiff mix who, despite his size, was a scaredy cat, to put it bluntly. He had loads of trust issues and insecurities that bubbled to the surface on walks. If a stranger or dog got within ten feet of him, Rufus would begin barking and lunging like a madman. However, he wasn't actually wanting to attack. He was scared and reacting the only way he knew how, by fighting.

Behaviors Associated with Fight Include:

- Hair standing up from the shoulder forward
- Standing tall, weight forward on front legs, tail high and staring at other dogs
- Standing his ground, and not moving
- Guarding food, toys, or territory against people and dogs
- Dislike of being petted or groomed
- Lying in front of doorways or cupboards and refusing to move
- Growling at people or dogs when he feels his space is being violated
- Putting his head over the shoulder of another dog

Like Fight, Flight is pretty-self-explanatory. Winnie had had a charmed life, unlike many of the dogs I train. No trauma, no abuse and no neglect for this little girl. But despite her seemingly easy life, Winnie was, like Rufus, insecure and untrusting by nature. Unlike Rufus, however, Winnie did not meet her fear head-on. Rather, she cowered, avoided eye contact and eventually would squirm between her owner's legs if the threat didn't subside.

"Sometimes she even runs the other way as fast and hard as she can," her dad told me. "She hits the end of the leash so hard I'm worried she's going to hurt herself one of these days."

Behaviors Associated with Flight Include:

- Hair that goes up the full length of the body, not just at the neck
- Hiding or running away from a new situation
- A dislike of being touched by strangers
- General lack of confidence
- Urinating when being greeted by a stranger or the owner
- Making themselves small
- Flattening of the body with tail tucked when greeted by people or other dogs
- Practicing avoidance by cowering away, not making eye contact and generally trying to avoid the situation.

Scaredy Cats...Er, Dogs

While we thoroughly cover the fight reaction in Chapter 6, I figured it would behoove us to cover those dogs that exhibit strong flight instincts. Before we begin, ask yourself this: Is your dog's fear something you need him to get over? Does it negatively impact your daily life and his? Or is it something you can live with because it happens rarely or you can avoid triggers? This behavior is fairly easy to pick up on by observing your dog's body language. Most dogs with a fear-based flight impulse start by making themselves small, crouching to the ground. They will try to hide behind you or in between your legs. These are the most common and most obvious signs that your dog is scared and looking to bolt. The first thing to remember, despite how pitiful and helpless he may look, is not to coddle him. It may be hard to refrain from picking him up in an attempt to soothe his nerves, but this reaction is counterproductive. Affection only serves to reward behaviors, so coddling him will simply reinforce and enable his fear. Don't become his security blanket – it sends the wrong message. Unlike with people, we cannot verbally console our dogs, explaining to them everything is OK and that they're not in danger. Thus, affection does not serve the same purpose as with a human. Calm leadership is the most effective way to handle a fearful dog. The more he trusts you, the more he'll trust fear-inducing situations, new people and so on. You cannot force a fearful dog – in most cases, this will simply cause him to shut down or become more stressed and scared.

Redirection and changing his association are the best routes to take. Because dogs only focus on one thing at a time, redirecting his attention is the most effective way to shift his mindset away from whatever is triggering his fear. You can do this by revisiting your foundation commands which we'll cover in Chapter 5 – for instance, put him in a Sit or Down-Stay then reward him with a treat. Another option is to turn and walk the other way – out of sight, out of mind. A physical redirection will provide him with new sights and smells. Many fearful dogs simply freeze. It's like a mental block, but redirecting his body will help thaw out his brain. Because dogs only think about one thing at a time, if you get his body moving, his mind will follow. Redirection causes his mind to reset and click back into gear. It also helps to change his association to whatever is causing him fear. If he is fearful around new people, try using treats so he'll begin to associate strangers with something positive, rather than with stress and fear. You will notice the change immediately in his body language; his muscles will loosen, he'll regain a normal stance, and he'll begin walking normally again. Once his body language shifts away from indicating fear, you may then give him affection. After all, the fear has subsided, so you're no longer rewarding that emotion.

It is always important to understand your dog – his likes, dislikes, bugaboos, quirks. But in cases of fear-based reactions, it's especially helpful to really know his triggers. Honing in on what causes him stress allows you to act and react accordingly. Perhaps it's a barking dog on your normal walking path. If you're aware of that being a trigger, you can either adjust your route or be prepared to respond accordingly as you approach. Fall back onto your foundation, letting your dog know what you expect from him – this will decrease some of his fear, as he'll understand his role. If I've said it once, I've said it a thousand times, the key to success lies in understanding and communication. Expectations must be clearly communicated, not merely assumed. This will provide your dog with a sense of security.

I once worked with a dog named Lexy, a 10-pound terrier mix who exhibited extreme shyness when it came to meeting new people. She would cower to the ground and hide between her owner's legs. It was especially strange given how confident and secure Lexy seemed the rest of the time. Helping Lexy through her shyness ended up being easier than you might think. The key with a shy dog is to give them space and allow them to warm up in their own time.

Now, when Lexy meets a stranger, her owner asks the new person to avoid making eye contact. The new person essentially ignores Lexy, taking the attention and pressure off of her. Lexy is given the time and space to sniff, investigate, and familiarize herself on her terms. Now, with just these minor tweaks, Lexy is typically at the new person's feet, looking for love and attention, within five minutes. It all boils down to slow introductions and gradual exposure. Consider someone who's fearful of spiders – you wouldn't just submerge them in a tank of tarantulas to get them over this fear, would you? Of course not – you'd slowly expose them to spiders, bit by bit, little by little. The same goes for helping fearful dogs conquer their issues.

Dogs are naturally inquisitive and want to explore; however, many of them just want to do it in their own timeframe. It's important to understand this about your dog and allow them the freedom to nose around in their own way. If exploration leads to fear, however, you can redirect your dog's attention, shift his mind away from fear then try revisiting the situation with a new mindset. Often times, a different mindset elicits a different reaction.

As owners, we love creating elaborate backstories for our dogs. "My dog is scared of garden gnomes because his old owner used to chase him around with one." Chances are, the tales we weave are probably not accurate. There's a misconception that all fearful dogs were once abused. This is simply not so. Some dogs are just fearful. And while our impulse is to pick him up and sing him a soothing lullaby, this response will only exacerbate his issues. If you want a well-balanced, less fearful dog, take an active role in guiding him past his fear. Identify the cause then formulate the best method of redirection that will allow his brain to reset and his mind to wander away from fear and an instinct to flee.

All animals Are Created Equal but Some are More Equal Than Others

Like us, dogs are instinctively wired to live as part of a family unit, and within every family – be it human or canine – there is an underlying social order. Sure, we strive for concrete equality, but in reality, each of our social groups consists of a subtle food chain. There are leaders, there are followers, and there's everyone in between. Though we might not like to talk about or acknowledge this, as it frays the seams of equality, every group, partnership and social dynamic possesses a slight power discrepancy, and the same is true for dogs.

Within the canine family unit, the leader is the animal that makes the rest feel safe through a balance of calm assertiveness. While in our society we elect our leaders, dogs instinctively gravitate towards theirs – typically the animal that exudes balanced energy and leads with confidence. Because nobody wants to be led by a weakling or a Genghis Canine – neither dogs nor humans – the head of a dog family exhibits both kindness and assertiveness, depending on the situation. He is the one the others look to for safety, food, and stability. And while other members of the group play vital roles and possess unique and necessary strengths, they all follow the leader.

Problems in this system only arise when there is no strong leader to follow, as this causes confusion, insecurity, and instability. Just consider the implications to our own society if it were void of leaders, government, and bosses. In theory it might sound ideal, but it would inevitably create significant turmoil and chaos. We would feel vulnerable and insecure without the feelings of safety and security our social structure provides.

Dogs gravitate to a leader based solely upon merit and credibility. They are cut-and-dry in this respect. There are no negotiations, back-room deals, or exceptions. They either trust and respect you, or they don't. If you can't walk the walk and talk the talk, then your dog will not look to you as his leader. His trust and respect will wane. Ask yourself, how much genuine credibility do you have with your dog? How seriously does he take you as a leader?

When looking to you for leadership, your dog doesn't consider factors like wealth, education, physical appearance, or social status. He merely looks to whoever provides him with his basic necessities, possesses a calm, confident attitude, and lays down the law in a way he understands. Your dog instinctively does what's best for his survival – and if you won't step up to the plate, then he'll find someone who will, even if he has to do it himself.

Because of this, your dog may act differently with each family member, depending on the relationship. To your dog, everyone in the family has a purpose that's determined by his relationship with them. Therefore, he will approach each of you in a different way. Have you noticed that he listens to you more consistently than to your spouse, or vice versa? Perhaps he seeks out one of your children when he wants to play or get fed. In his mind, you each have a distinct role – and it's especially important that he understands his.

While certain dogs – like certain humans — may strive for control and leadership, this is not necessarily the best role for them. In these instances, that individual needs to be shown there is a place within the group better suited for his skills and abilities. After all, being the leader can be stressful and brings with it a great deal of responsibility. Your dog would much rather you take the lead, allowing him to get on with being cute.

If, however, he is not confident in your ability to lead, he will feel the need to take over – and that's when unwanted behaviors ensue.

Tank was a stunning, jet black German Shepherd I worked with just a few months before finishing this book. He was truly a show stopper. Smart, beautiful but controlling – that was Tank. However, he didn't know his place nor did he look to his mom for leadership. She'd yet to earn that position and therefore, Tank had taken over. Due to his particular disposition, my approach was for his mom to take on the role of drill sergeant. Tank needed a very assertive, structured and consistent leader in order to quell his control tendencies. Once she began tackling his issues from this approach, Tank did as any good soldier and fell in line. He became confident in her leadership role and no longer felt it necessary to take matters into his own paws. during a follow-up phone call, his mom regaled me with how much Tank enjoyed his new structure and routine. "He's so dialed in, always looking at me as if to say, 'What's our new mission, Sergeant?'"

It is essential that your dog not only knows his role, but also knows he can count on you to ensure his survival. So long as you can competently provide him with what he needs and let your dog know you have things under control, he'll happily fall into his rightful place. In order to accomplish this, you must first have a strong relationship with your pet – he's not merely going to take your word for it.

Nature vs. Nurture

A scorpion and frog meet on a riverbank. Stop me if you've heard this one. The scorpion says, "Hey, you can swim! Will you give me a ride across the river?"

The frog scoffs, "Of course not! You'll sting me and I'll drown."

Shaking his head, the scorpion insists, "I won't, I won't. For if you drown, I'll also die."

The frog considers this for a moment. "Ok, hop on," and the two take off across the river.

Right as they reach the middle of the river, the frog suddenly feels a sharp sting in his back. "Ow! You stung me, but why? Now you shall die, as well!"

As they go under, the scorpion says, "Sorry, it's just in my nature."

Nature and nurture go hand-in-hand when sculpting a dog's personality and temperament. While you can set him up for success, know and understand him, recognize his triggers, communicate your expectations and provide him a loving, structured environment, there will be parts of disposition you just can't control — those determined by nature.

Very recently I worked with two shepherd sisters. They came from the same litter, had the same puppyhood and were even adopted into the same family. Their lives had been identical. One of the sisters, Franny, was incredibly affectionate with both her adoptive mom and dad. She had few issues and pretty much trotted through life happy as a clam. Zooey, the other sister, however, exhibited massive trust issues towards her dad - even having bitten him a time or two. He'd had the same interactions with each, never favoring one over the other. The environment and circumstances were the exact same for both girls; yet, they had very different personalities, temperaments and triggers. These ladies are a prime example of the role nature plays.

Conversely, in the years I spent working in rescue, I experienced the power of nurture when working with dogs in foster homes. I would get called in to the same home multiple times to work with a dog on the same issue — to no avail. We would then make the decision to switch the dog to a new home and wouldn't you know it? The behaviors would melt away.

You need to account for both nature and nurture when tackling any issue plaguing your dog. With nature, you must consider your dog's genetic makeup, and subsequent limitations. Keep your expectations realistic. Take him as far as you can and then focus on managing the rest around his natural born disposition. Likewise, make sure your environment is set up in a way to nurture his particular personality in a way that sets him up for success.

CHAPTER 5

Let's Get to Work

Building the Foundation

It's first important to understand that while we may try to relate to our dogs on a human level – talking to them, toting them around with us on errands, and even dressing them up – we must remember, they are wired a bit differently than we are. Because their minds are always in the present, different actions have different meanings to them. Cuddling a dog when he's fearful doesn't send the same message as holding a child when she's scared. Dogs don't plan for the future. They don't concern themselves with thoughts of retirement and what's to come down the road. They don't linger in the past, wondering what might have been and waxing poetic about the good old days. Our dogs live in the now, the present. They are masters at gelling to their current environment and their behaviors are dictated by instincts – namely, their instinct to survive. By nature, dogs are opportunists; constantly determining what they can get away with, pushing boundaries, and testing us to see which behaviors we'll let fly. Until you set the parameters for them, they will test, push and nudge, searching for their role in the family dynamic – and for structure and routine.

Because dogs are structure and routine-oriented, they create strong associations – both good and bad – that gradually become habitual behaviors. When you go into the kitchen and open the refrigerator, your dog likely runs, full-speed after you, tail wagging – do you break off a piece of whatever it is you're eating and share it with him? Or, when your tiny dog stands at your feet, barking and pawing at you, do you pick him up? If your answer is yes, then it only makes sense he'll continue these behaviors because he associates them with getting exactly what he wants – a tasty morsel or prime spot on your lap. This is even the case in scenarios you are not directly affecting. For instance, when you're walking down the sidewalk and your dog begins barking at a stranger walking towards you, the moment that person passes you by and is gone, your dog feels as though his barking directly caused that result. He then forms a strong cause-and-effect association that can become a habit. This is just how he is wired, but it's important to understand so we, as owners, can become aware of how our actions may influence his associations and consequently, his habitual behaviors. Or, in the case of the stranger danger scenario, we can understand why he continues to bark and lunge, despite our best efforts to get him to cut it out. Then, we can find a new approach for dealing with this situation.

Our dogs also receive a powerful adrenaline rush when lashing out and misbehaving. Certain things – new people, other dogs, prey, animals, etc. – act as triggers, causing strong emotional and physical reactions within our dogs. In that moment, reacting to that trigger makes him feel better, more in control. Think of your own triggers, we all have them – certain people, topics, or even associations that stress you out, make you anxious, and result in strong reactions within you. We all have hot button issues within our own lives, sensitive topics that hit a nerve and possibly cause us to lose our cool for a moment. Maybe your parents fought incessantly when you were growing up and now the sound of yelling causes you anxiety, triggering an emotional and physical reaction. Or maybe a certain song reminds you of your first love and any time you hear it, you feel sadness, nostalgia, or a sense of loss. We have these strong emotions despite our ability to logically think them through and stop ourselves – essentially, we know better. Dogs, on the other hand, do not have this capability, so maintain realistic expectations and cut him a little slack when he reacts instinctively. After all, he doesn't even have a therapist to call. Anxiety and stress are powerful physical reactions; they cause our bodies to take over, leaving us to search for any means necessary to make that feeling go away. Our dogs experience similar reactions to triggers; however, for us, these associations tend to be far more complex than they are for our dogs. On the flip side, however, we have the ability to intelligently and logically calm ourselves down, or be pacified by someone else talking it out with us. Our dogs do not have this luxury. We cannot sit them down and explain that everything will be alright. We can't reason with them. Many of the methods we tend to use are equivalent to a friend or family member simply saying, "Get over it," in regards to our stressful and anxiety-inducing associations. It is not that simple. We must work with our dog to change his association, thereby reducing the trigger effect it has on him. Until we do this, he'll continue to bark, lunge, chew, and nip because in that moment, it provides him a cathartic release.

I once worked with a girl who had three terrier mixes – each with its own brand of Napoleonic neuroses. Anytime she walked them through her neighborhood, the trio would go nuts, barking and lunging, at every passer-by, dog, squirrel and leaf in their path. No matter what she tried to quell their fury, nothing worked. She couldn't figure out why her dogs were so sweet, calm and even friendly inside, but once on their leashes and outdoors, they completely changed – it was like Dr. Jekyll and Mr. Hound, multiplied by three. Because these walks were such a fundamental part of their daily routine, they began to anticipate these opportunities. Eventually, not just the walks were ingrained in their day-to-day structure, but the anticipation, the chance to misbehave and experience that physical and emotional release. In situations like this, the anticipation builds and dogs can become addicted to it, like an adrenaline junkie. The reward was two-fold, both physical, through the release, and emotional, the cause-and-effect nature of their behavior. For this particular client, it became a vicious cycle. They'd be enjoying their walk, a person would approach, her dogs would go nuts, the person would walk away. She felt like there was little she could do to break this cycle. Her dogs were being rewarded in a way she didn't think she could control. The power of association is strong and the key in a situation like this is to change the association. Once you understand how these behaviors become habits, it is then easier to switch gears and create new habitual behaviors and more positive associations.

My ultimate goal is to teach you the most effective ways to communicate with your dog. Like in any relationship, communication is key. This process begins by building a strong, solid foundation atop of which all subsequent training will stand. This foundation will enable you and your dog to build mutual respect and trust. Think of it as an investment in your dog; put in the time and effort to create this bond and watch it pay dividends down the road when you need to set boundaries, change a behavior or reward an action. With the right relationship, your dog will actually comply due to the trust and respect between you. As this relationship grows and the equity in your dog increases, this behavior and dynamic will become the norm over time.

Once the foundation is in place, your dog will relinquish control and you can switch him from Prey Drive into Pack Drive. He will begin to feel safe, secure, and calm, as he trusts that you have things under control – no matter what arises. And that is the main point of the foundation – to serve as a safety net for you to fall back on during stressful situations. Once you have your dog's trust and respect, he'll then feel secure in letting you handle matters. He'll settle into his role, relinquish control and just get on with being cute. Think of the foundation, the relationship you share with your dog, as a platform to build on. You're laying the groundwork, gaining his trust and respect, and creating a platform you can fall back on – or default to – when the wicket gets a little sticky.

Working with your dog to build this foundation also gives him a job. Dogs like to work, it engages them mentally and physically. Teaching him to Sit, Stay, and Come serves multiple purposes – not only does he learn valuable commands you can use in a variety of situations, it also reinforces your role as leader. And lastly, during this time, your dog will be dialed in and engaged, he'll feel a sense of purpose, understand what's expected of him, and gain mental stimulation – which is as important as physical activity. And I bet he'll even enjoy it.

So, how do we build this relationship?

While my goal is to go beyond simply teaching you training tricks, there are several fundamental commands your dog should learn. This is not so much because of the commands themselves – though they are instrumental in having an obedient dog – but mainly because of the relationship this process will build between you two. By working on the basics, your dog will begin to see you as his leader, which will increase his trust and security. This will then enable you to tackle larger and more severe behavioral issues more efficiently and effectively. The fundamentals also allow you an opportunity to begin slowly, setting your dog up for success. As time goes on, these commands will become routine, giving you the opportunity to venture into deeper waters. But without this initial foundation to default back to when needed, any future endeavors will most likely fail and possibly set you back a few steps.

I highly recommend using treats and positive reinforcement techniques to begin teaching your dog. Bribery is your best friend. If your dog isn't motivated by regular treats, bring out the big guns — hot dogs, cheese, whatever gets his mouth watering. High value bribes are also effective in areas with lots of stimulation. By motivating and rewarding your dog, you're teaching him new behaviors and laying the foundation. The end goal is to remove the treats altogether and for him to obey because you damn well say so. This method will allow you to feed two birds with one seed – you're teaching your dog while simultaneously gaining his trust. When you tell him to go lie down, you're not only getting him to do as you want, you're also building your relationship with him – earning his respect and gaining his trust in you. While treats are important in the beginning, you don't want to become too reliant on them. Gradually you will want to decrease your use of treats – this way, he learns to act accordingly because you say so, not simply because you have a piece of cheese in your hand. The best way to wean him off treats is in low-stimulation settings – until he has this down, continue to reward him with high-value treats, those morsels he loves most, in distracting and stressful environments. So, in your home, your own backyard or wherever he is most dialed in, begin using treats sporadically – every other time you give a command, reward him. Then, every second time, every third time, etc. You want to mix it up so he never really knows when a treat might be given. Eventually, you should be able to stop using them altogether. The treats are simply to teach the command – once he's learned, he should act on it strictly because you damn well say so. After all, it's now a command.

There are a couple tricks that carry out through each of these commands. First, when working with your dog, always keep his leash on – even if you're in the house. When teaching your dog these initial commands, you will utilize both physical and verbal control in tandem; meaning, when you say the command, this is you exhibiting verbal control, but then you will also use the leash to give your dog physical instruction. Choose a calm environment free of distractions and have your bribery ready. I typically advise owners to start by working with their dog inside the house. Dogs are usually most comfortable in their own home and this setting provides the optimal setting for your dog to be dialed in with you. You should be able to keep his attention for a longer period of time, as there won't be the same potential for distraction as there would be outside. You need to make sure your dog is dialed in and that his command responses are solid and on point. I once worked with a client and his three-legged pit, Calvin. Calvin was a pretty obedient dog – inside. But because his behaviors were not yet habits and his commands were not ingrained, once his owner walked him out the door and onto the busy, distraction-riddled streets of Los Angeles, Calvin became unmanageable. It is so important that commands are solidly instilled in your dog indoors – this will increase the potential for good behavior outside of the home.

When teaching your dog, say the command once calmly and assertively. Don't mistake frustration or anger with an assertive tone – these are very different and your dog knows it. Calm yet assertive is the tonal sweet spot. I sometimes advise owners to video themselves giving commands in order to ensure they are conveying the right calm and assertive energy. I once worked with a client who thought she was doing this, but after watching herself on video, she realized she was far meeker than she'd thought.

Do not repeat the command. If your dog obeys, give him a treat. However, if he doesn't, physically put him into the command – for example, put him into a Sit position by applying upward pressure on the leash while pushing down on his booty with your hand – repeat the verbal command and give him a treat. Only use as much pressure as you need to get the desired results. Always maintain eye contact and say the command assertively – calm, but assertive is key. In other words, say it like you really mean it. Don't wait for a long, loving gaze before releasing him or moving on. Eye contact can occur in a fleeting split second – watch for it closely. Once you receive it, move forward. If he is resistant to giving eye contact, then look for other signs he's dialed in – calm, relaxed energy. This is as meaningful as eye contact, so take it and proceed.

Dogs create strong associations – both good and bad. However, once you understand this and learn to wield it properly, the Power of Association can greatly work in your favor. This is why we use treats to teach our dogs to Sit. As we continue this technique, they begin to associate obeying with reward. On the converse, negative associations can work against you if you don't change them. Some dogs have bad associations to certain collars – like a prong – because they've been used incorrectly or excessively. This is a challenge when you purchase a prong, intending to use it properly as a training tool, only to discover the mere sight of it exacerbates your dog's issues. Once you have altered his association to a trigger and he's dialed in and engaged, this is a sign he's deferring to you. He's looking at you asking, "What should I do next?" But it all starts with changing his association when it comes to negative triggers. I've mentioned before people who are scared of spiders – rather than dunking them in a tank of tarantulas to get them past their fear, the effective tactic would be to slowly expose them to spiders. This allows them to gradually change their association and to see there's nothing to fear. Desensitizing works just as effectively with dogs as people. Often times, when dogs misbehave, it's due to an insecurity and fear. There are several key components to changing this – altering your dog's association combined with a strong relationship between you and your dog. This chapter focuses on that relationship – by laying a solid foundation, you will gain your dog's trust and respect, automatically lessening his fears and insecurities. These training techniques are nothing new or revolutionary; however, they are often underused by owners. And yet, they are an owner's best friend.

So, stand up, grab your dog's leash and get ready to work. This section will be easier to digest if you do what's written, rather than only read it. Go to a quiet, distraction-free environment and let's get to work. It's a win/win – you'll get what you want from your dog and he'll get what he needs from you.

Sit

Body language matters. Stand up! And as you practice this command, even take a step towards your dog to further establish your assertive posture.

With a treat in hand, stand in front of your dog while maintaining eye contact. Eye contact is important, as it shows you have his full attention – it ensures you two are dialed in to one another.

Show him the treat so he knows what he's working for, then close your fist around it.

Say the command in an assertive tone.

Lift the treat and move it upwards – your dog will follow it with his head and then body, until he plops into a seated position. At this point, give him his reward and repeat the command.

Only give him the treat if this command is done correctly – the first time.

Only say, "Sit" once. Don't say it over and over. If he's not doing it, redirect his attention – as if to reboot him. Take him on a quick walk or call him to you – anything to reset his attention. Dogs think about just one thing at a time.

If he doesn't go back into a seated position, apply a little upward pressure on the leash combined with your hand on his rump pushing downward – this will encourage him and his momentum. As he goes back, let off the pressure. Just apply enough pressure to get him to comply.

After you've done this a few times with success, begin using a treat only every other time, then every other other time and so on until your dog sits without needing the motivation. This moves you from trust to respect.

Stay

First instruct your dog to sit. Once seated, use a calm but assertive tone and tell him to Stay.

It often helps to use a visual cue here, as well – like a traffic cop's "Stop!" hand signal.

Take one step back and then one step forward. If he stays as he was told, give him the treat. Once you're able to do this without him moving from his spot, begin to increase the distance.

Remember to start off slowly – only make him stay for a couple seconds at first. As this command becomes more firmly established, increase the time you make him stay and the distance between you.

Then come back, give him the treat and release him with, "OK" or a tap on your leg – any signal that lets him know he can move.

Practice with boundaries – for example, have him stay in the kitchen while you move to another room. This will extend his threshold.

Come

Once you've gotten your dog to sit and stay, it's time for come. Your dog's recall training needs to be very strong; so strong, in fact, that it works even when your dog is distracted. The stronger his recall, the more effectively you can use redirection to reset his mind. In the meantime, it's crucial you build a strong recall within your dog and that he knows when you say "Come," he needs to do so.

In order to recall your dog, get him to sit and stay. Then take several steps back, but rather than returning to him to give him his treat, stay where you are. Put a treat in your hand and close your fist – this way he's targeting your hand instead of the treat. This will come in handy as you teach him to come whether you have a bribe or not.

Crouch down and make your body language inviting. Keep his leash in your hand and in a welcoming tone, give the verbal command, "Come." When he obeys, reward him and repeat the word Come.

If he does not come at first, use the leash to remind him, by guiding him towards you. Be sure to use his name only to get his attention, not as a substitute for the command.

As this becomes more instilled in him, make the distance between you two larger and larger. You can even get a longer leash to practice extending his recall ability.

Be in tune with your own energy and that of your dog. Perhaps an inviting tone will help encourage him towards you. Though, for some dogs, a more assertive voice may get the message across better. Stay subdued to prevent him becoming overly excited and hurling himself at you as he approaches.

"Come" is a great command for redirecting your dog and refocusing his attention to you. If you're walking down the street and a squirrel or cat gets his attention, use "Come" to dial him back in with you.

Let's Go

This command comes in handy when your dog is lagging behind on a walk – or if you simply want him to move along. With Let's Go, you will also use a physical command along with the verbal – a little pop of the leash will aid in communicating to your dog what you're wanting him to do.

As with the other commands, you'll use a physical and verbal command in tandem. So, a gentle tug of the leash will accompany you saying "Let's Go!" in an assertive tone.

Depending on your dog's personality, you may need to use an animated tone to get the results you want. With others, a calmer voice may ensure he doesn't come leaping and bounding towards you.

You can also use a hand signal or tap your leg.

Your own forward momentum will serve as the bulk of the physical element.

Remember, the end goal is to get him to obey with simply the verbal command.

Leave It

"Leave it" will become your best friend on walks. Most dogs have a tendency to become distracted when overwhelmed with all the distractions the great outdoors has to offer. This command is useful at times when your dog is unfocused, picking up items you'd rather not have to touch to force him to part with and even if your dog begins to bark or lunge.

The moment you see his attention go to something — like a squirrel, another dog or a piece of trash on the ground — correct him. This way, you're correcting his thought before it becomes an action.

In unison, pop the leash and say, "Leave it!" in your now expert tone. As you work on this command, you should come to a point when the physical correction is no longer needed. Give him a treat, turn, and walk the other way or command him to sit; dogs only think about one thing at a time, so giving him an alternative task or focal point will snap his attention back to you.

Place Mat

Designate a dog bed or mat as your dog's "place." Take them over to it and tell him to sit. Once seated, give them the command "Down." To get them to lie down, show him a treat in your hand and take it down to the bed. Then move it in an L shape away from your dog. As he follows, he will slide into a laying position.

Then place the treat on the bed between his front paws. This way, he'll begin associating his bed with treats. Command him to Stay. Then take a step back, a step forward and give him the treat.

Then tell him to Stay again. "Stay" is the only command you may repeat because it reinforces what he's already doing.

Once your dog is comfortable with this, begin increasing your distance little by little. When backing up, always face your dog and maintain eye contact.

Practice this in increments throughout the day. Five minutes here, five minutes there. Try walking around your house, coming back to repeat the command and give him another treat. Keep it realistic, however. Don't go take a shower and expect to come back and find him still in that position.

When you've put your dog in a Down Stay position on the place mat, you must go over and physically release him. This way he'll know he is to stay there until you walk over and give him permission.

In a Down-Stay, you may use a verbal cue like, "OK" or tap your leg in order to release him. However, Down Stays must be actively released once you're back next to him.

Place mat training is important because it teaches your dog a Down-Stay position. Once your dog has this down in your calm training environment, you can then begin utilizing this command in other areas - other rooms, in the backyard, on walks, etc. If he has trouble learning it outside his comfort zone, try taking whatever you're using as his place mat to these various locations - this way he'll begin forming the association between Down-Stay and these areas. I utilize this technique often with my dog Duchess, who becomes overly-stimulated and very excitable on walks. But because her Down-Stay command is so strong, I can put her in this position to regain control of the situation.

Crate Training

I often hear people say they don't want to crate their dog, that it seems cruel to confine him to a cage. Though this may seem understandable, it's actually inaccurate. When a mom puts her baby in a crib, does that seem cruel? Of course not - a crib is a safe, cozy place for the baby to sleep and relax, right? Well, the same goes for a crate. A dog's crate is essentially his palace—a space that's entirely his own, something we all need. It's his comfy den where he can decompress and unwind from the stresses of dog life.

Let me ask you a question. When you're asleep or away from the house, what do you want from your dog? Most likely, your answer is, "I want him to lie around and sleep." Otherwise, he could get into mischief – after all, idle paws… When a dog is left out when you're away or asleep, you are giving him too much freedom. One way dogs are not like us is in this instance. While we love freedom, dogs do not handle it quite so well. For most a dog, being left to roam free when home alone creates anxiety. He feels he must take control, patrol the home and protect it. This is when things like chewing and barking occur. Putting them in a crate, however, gives them the opportunity to relax and snooze. It also communicates to them your expectations – do nothing. This is his time to relax, this is his own personal place where he can nap and take a load off. In turn, your dog can drift off into puppy dreams secure in knowing you have things under control.

Crate training your dog is also a useful tool when it comes to potty training. So long as you choose the appropriate size crate, your dog will not want to go to the bathroom in there; thus, he'll learn to hold it. There is absolutely nothing cruel about a tool that provides your dog safety, security, comfort and structure and routine – and a home all his own.

The Basics:

- First off, you can crate train a dog of any age. So no more, "He's too old to adjust" excuses! I once worked with a dog named Leann, a super sweet pit mix who stole the heart of everyone she met. However, the crate was her Achilles' heel. She hated it and broke out of three different crates, destroying them despite her petite size. Because she was three years old, her parents figured she was just too old to learn new tricks. But once I helped them to change her association to the crate, we had her happily trained within three days.

- Your dog's association to the crate is key. Crate training should be part of the daily routine; it helps with separation anxiety, destructive tendencies and barking. Keep your dog's association with his crate positive – never use it as a punishment.
- Make the crate part of your training routine. You know that whole slew of commands we just learned? Practice them while he's in the crate, as well.
- When choosing a crate, make sure you select one that's large enough for him to stand up and turn around; however, it should not be so large that he can potty in one corner and then lie down a fair distance away from that spot. Plastic crates tend to be more secure than wired ones.
- Don't put water in the crate; this is a spilling hazard. Or, your dog will guzzle it down then be stuck in his crate needing to pee.
- I don't recommend leaving your dog crated for more than 4-5 hours. In fact, do not leave him in nearly this long in the beginning. Start off small, in increments, until you work up to 4-5 hours.
- Work on the foundation commands – Sit, Stay, and Come – in the crate. Just as you worked on them inside, outside, in different rooms, and settings, you'll want to do the same in his crate. It's simply a new place – not a new opportunity for him to take control.
- Stock his crate with a comfy bed or blanket, his favorite toy and maybe even a bone. Make it his palace, his own space – a place for him to relax, sleep, and generally chill out. Some dogs find comfort from their owner's scent, so try tossing in a T-shirt or other article of clothing that smells like you.
- Place the crate in a quiet, relaxing environment – such as the bedroom. It should be associated with sleep and peace. Do not place it

by the front door or in a busy area of the house. He'll never be able to relax. Plus, he associates higher traffic rooms with excitement, walks, playtime, etc.

- Introduce a dog to his crate little by little. While you're at home, put him in for very short periods of time – just a few minutes. Do this numerous times and slowly extend the time he's in there.
- If he whines, cries, or barks, give him a verbal correction. Do not let him out of the crate until he's calm and quiet.
- Practice leaving; go out the front door and close it. Then come back in and so long as he's quiet, let him out. Build up the time.
- Look for triggers that spark anxiety in him – like you picking up your keys. If this action causes him to become stressed, trick him. Pick up your keys and simply move them to another surface. This will help desensitize him to those catalysts.
- Your dog should sleep in his crate at night. Make it like his bedroom – you can even cover it to make it cozier, more den-like. But make sure, if you put a sheet over it, that it's taut. You don't want him to be able to pull the sheet into his crate and tear it up when he should just be relaxing.
- Like a baby with its crib, your dog may resist the crate at first. Keep it on your terms and don't give in to him. He'll come around and learn to love having a place that's all his. He'll also gain a great deal from the structure and routine it provides.
- When you're putting him in or taking him out of the crate, be matter of fact. Keep your tone level and your energy calm.
- Be aware, anxious dogs may chew on their bedding or other items you place in the crate. Some dogs may also try to break out – make sure it's completely closed. If they think they can escape, they'll just keep trying.

Using the Foundation to Correct Common Issues

Leash Issues

Leash Issues can cover a wide variety of behaviors including:

- Pulling
- Dragging
- Stalling, falling back and refusal to walk
- Lunging
- Barking at people or other animals
- Jumping

These are all symptoms and while they may appear to be rooted in aggression, they sometimes stem from over-excitement and over-stimulation. Leash issues usually stem from either Prey or Defense Drive. Your dog just wants to get to the source of his drive. The leash, in these cases, can work against you if you're not prepared with a correction or redirection strategy. Because the leash restrains your dog, his excitement just continues to build, perpetuating his desire to get free. The trick is to teach him that he'll receive everything he wants once he's in a calm, relaxed state of mind. But until then, he won't get anything.

The most common complaints I hear from owners involves issues on the leash – does your dog pull, bark, lunge, bob and weave attempting to say, "Hello" to every passer-by, and stop to sniff or eat every piece of trash you see? If so, you're not alone. Certain dogs see walks on the leash as an opportunity to take control and become unmanageable. The key to stopping these behaviors is two-fold; you first need the right tools then the most effective method.

First off, if you're using a retractable leash – or FlexiLeash – get rid of it immediately. These leashes enable dogs to run all over, control the walk, and generally become out of control. You want to use a standard six-foot leash. No, you're not stripping your dog of his freedom – you're taking back control and actually increasing your dog's safety on walks. If you have a big dog, I advise using a double-handed leash, where you have a loop at the top and one down closer to where it connects to the collar.

Next, lose the harness. Harnesses encourage pulling and will give your dog the ability run wild on walks. Essentially, harnesses strip you of any control. There may be an element of trial and error involved, as you find the right walking collar for your dog, but there are many to choose from. You can use a Martingale collar – this tool does not choke the dog, but it does tighten when he pulls, correcting his behavior. There are also prong collars which apply more pressure. These are good for large dogs who prove especially stubborn and resistant to correction. Then there are Haltis. These loop around the dog's snout, allowing you to control him from his head rather than his neck. Go for the point of least resistance. Which tool best suits your dog? Which one is the most comfortable with? We covered this in Chapter 1, so refresh your memory if needed.

I once worked with a dog named Pinky who had been over-corrected with a prong collar. They triggered stress in him, rendering this tool ineffective. During our session, I switched to a Halti, which gave me control without making him anxious. Once we got him managed on the walk and used to this new collar, I was then able to reintroduce the prong collar. I had changed his association to the walking tools, replacing negative with positive. Use the tool that works best for your dog and causes the least disruption for him.

Once you have the right collar and leash, it's time to get walking. Essentially, the walk begins before you even leave the house. This is when you're setting the energy for your outing. As you leash up your dog, make sure his energy is calm. Default back to the foundation – make sure he's dialed in with you, have him give you eye contact and sit before you put on his walking collar and leash. Set the stage before ever opening the front door – this energy will carry out into your walk.

Once you're on the walk, fall back on your foundation training – Sit, Stay, Come, eye contact and so on. However, the key for peaceful walks is to get your dog to follow you – and for this to become a habit. For example, if you're walking north, do a 180-degree turn away from your dog and begin walking south. Get him to follow you. Whatever he wants to do, do the opposite. You should be able to do a 180-degree turn into or away from him and he will simply follow you. When you turn into him, he should allow this to happen then fall in behind you. Act as if you're playing Follow the Leader and guide him along by his leash. This also ensure follow through on his part. Not only does this demonstrate to him his role – as the follower – but you're also instilling in him good habits and breaking bad ones. On top of that, walks will now become both physically and mentally tiring for your dog. In order to fully wear out and relax a dog, both his body and mind should be exercised. These methods will accomplish this in one fell swoop.

Separation Anxiety

See the section above on Crate Training.

Often times, dogs exhibit separation anxiety because leaving them alone to roam free through the house causes them stress. They feel it is their job to guard and protect. By crate training them and leaving them in their palace when you're away from the house, you're communicating your expectations. You're letting them know that all you expect is for them to relax, sleep, and enjoy some quiet time. Crate training is an effective tool for combatting separation anxiety.

As you embark on remedying this issue, watch for triggers. Separation anxiety tends to build before you even leave the house. Maybe it's when you put on your shoes or grab your keys. Watch his body language and behavior.

When you see the trigger) take effect, go back to your Foundation. Remember, dogs only think about one thing at a time. Put him in Sit, Stay, Come mode and out of anxious mode.

Don't make a big deal out of leaving. It's part of your routine and doesn't need to be met with a big display of affection or baby talk.

Put him in his crate then fake him out. Do everything you'd do to get ready to leave, walk out the door then come back in a couple minutes later.

If you hear him bark or whine while you're still outside the door, bust him. Give him a verbal correction.

Then leave again. Do this a couple times if need be. This way, he won't know if you're actually leaving or not. Even go through this when you're not actually going anywhere. Go through the motions, crate him, leave then come back. Let him out of the crate if he's calm and behaving well.

Because leaving is part of life, make it part of your routine. Factor these steps into your training. The structure is where you'll leave your dog — in a crate, behind a baby gate, etc. — and you leaving is the routine.

Excessive Barking

First off, have realistic expectations. Dogs bark, it's natural and their way of communicating. A couple woofs when the doorbell rings are just his way of alerting you. It's then your job to speak Dog and say, "Thanks for letting me know. I've got it from here." So, if your dog gives a couple barks from time to time, cut him some slack. Excessive barking, however, is a different story.

If this occurs when you're not home, see the section on Crate Training.

If this occurs when you are home, use a spray bottle to give physical correction. Accompany this with "No" or "Leave it" as the verbal. Then work on the Place Mat training. Tell him to go to his place and put him in a Down-Stay. This says to your dog, "Thank you for letting me know, but I've got it from here."

You can also use a bark collar, such as a citronella collar or a remote collar. I advise going for the highest quality one possible. These are good because they give a physical correction as soon as the dog barks – and timing is always key.

Remember, however, dogs bark. This is just part of having a dog in your life. Excessive barking, however, is a sign of stress, over-stimulation and protectiveness.

Destructive Behaviors

If these occur while you're not at home, read the Crate Training section.

If, however, your dog is destroying things when you are home, first things first, keep an eye on him. Put his leash on, if necessary, so you can keep him close to you. This goes without saying, but pick up anything you may not want destroyed. If you catch him in the act, correct him immediately so he learns the rules. To help control his movements through the house, baby gate certain areas, giving him specific rooms he can and can't enter. Also, provide him with an alternative item to chew on. Take your shoe or sock or whatever it is he's destroying out of his mouth and replace it with one of his favorite toys. This will teach him which items are off limits and which are acceptable. And don't set him up to fail — if you know your dog's a chewer, don't leave your favorite shoes out then leave the house. That's entrapment!

Begging

First off, be realistic. I recently worked with a couple and their beagle mix. The wife was so annoyed because Jax would not stop begging at meal time.

"He just stands there, looking up at us," she said, pointing to a spot about three feet away from the dinner table.

I looked at her incredulously. "He stands here?" I said, moving to the area where she'd pointed.

"Yes! And just stares at us!"

"Does he whine? Bark? Try to steal your food?"

"No, he just stares."

I'm not exactly sure what she expected Jax to do — simply ignore the fact there's food in the vicinity? He's a dog. If it's that bothersome, then put him outside. But in the meantime, be realistic.

When it comes to begging for food, there needs to be consistency in the house. If your dog begs, chances are it's because someone has given him food. He's learned begging works. So make sure everyone in your house is on the same page. If the begging does not stop, you can remove your dog while you're eating; put him in his crate, in the backyard, or put him behind a baby gate. You can also put his leash on him and keep him close to you, but not close enough to beg. Sending him to his place mat is another good tactic, but only if your pup's Down-Stay command is really solid. Also consider feeding your dog at the same time you eat, this way he'll be distracted with his own food.

Jumping

Jumping is a pretty easy issue to fix. Nine times out of ten, a change in your approach and energy will stop this behavior. For instance, when you come home or have guests over, the dog should be completely ignored at first. If your dog jumps on you or guests then receives attention, like a pat on the head, his behavior is being rewarded. Even pushing him away can reinforce his excited mindset. However, if you completely ignore him, this will typically teach the dog that jumping does not get him the results he wants, and he'll stop. Even making eye contact or looking at the dog is interacting with him, so avoid these actions, as well. Wait until he's calm and relaxed, then give him a rub or allow people to give him attention — that way, you're rewarding the more tranquil mindset.

If you know someone is coming over, put on your dog's leash and revert to your Foundation commands. If he tends to jump more in one area — like near the front door — reclaim that area. Physically back him away from that space and put him into a sit. Remember, dogs only think about one thing at a time, so if he's focused on you and obeying your commands, jumping won't cross his mind.

Accidents in the House

Routine, routine, routine! If your dog is going potty in the house, first make sure you're taking him out enough. If he is emptying his bladder on your kitchen floor, chances are, he just really needed to go. So make sure you're giving him plenty of opportunities. I mean, could you hold it if you were only given two bathroom breaks a day? I doubt it. Also, limit his water if necessary.

If, however, your dog is marking inside the house, that's a different story. In this case, make sure his favorite spots to mark are kept very clean. I advise using Nature's Miracle or a strong, pet-specific cleaner like that. Move the furniture around so he cannot get to these spots. Regulate his food and water schedule and if you catch him in the act, use physical and verbal correction to communicate your expectations regarding this. It's extremely important to note, however, that you cannot correct him after the fact — this is just confusing to him. He won't understand why you're upset. Only if you literally see him squat and pee can you correct him right then and there. Do not return hours later and rub his nose in it – this communicates nothing to him.

A Few Reminders

- Dogs only focus on one thing at a time; however, this focus can change rapidly. "There's a cat! There's a squirrel! There's a car!" Because of this, it's important to start small and not try to do too much at once. Their attention spans are fleeting, so we're looking for quality rather than quantity. Instead of trying to push the limits of their focus, work within it.
- Work with your dog in the least stressful environment possible, with few distractions and stimulation. As I said, in your home is the best place at first, but even get more specific than that – perhaps the kitchen provides the fewest distractions or maybe he's calmest in your bedroom. Where ever he is the most focused and dialed in with you, start there; set you and your dog up to succeed.
- As you succeed and make steps forward, you can begin to up the ante and push his training threshold.
- Keep it matter-of-fact. When your dog obeys a command, give him a treat and move on. Don't begin overly praising or petting him. This changes and dilutes the energy and alters the dynamic. Whatever you did to get him to obey, keep it up.

- Make sure everything you do is on your terms. You're the entity in charge – always.
- Work with your dog in a low-stimulation area
- Don't over-do it; start off working with him in short spurts and build up the time as you go. For instance, when seeking eye contact, don't expect a long gaze. Dialed in and engaged eye contact just be fleeting, a split second – that is sufficient. Move on. If you're not getting eye contact, look for other indications that your dog is exuding calm, relaxed energy. This shows he is dialed in and engaged. You can then release him or move on.
- Use physical and verbal commands in tandem; tell him what you want him to do with an assertive tone, then use his leash to back it up physically. As time goes on, the goal is eventually to need only the verbal.
- Always leave on a positive note. Don't push it.
- Do whatever you can to set up yourself and your dog for success.
- Video yourself as you're working with your dog. This way, you can replay it and make sure you're projecting the assertive energy needed.
- Always remember, practice makes perfect – for better or worse. The key is to stop unwanted behaviors before they become learnt habits.
- Keep everything calm, controlled, and simple. So many owners try taking on too much too soon. They become frustrated and stressed. Breathe and simmer down. There's an element of trial-and-error to this process as you figure everything out; how your dog responds, how you're giving these commands. Should you be more assertive, less?

CHAPTER 6

The First Two Weeks

Whether he's eight weeks or eight years, the first two weeks you have a dog are the most important when it comes to laying down the foundation, communicating your expectations, and establishing everyone's role in the family. He is a blank slate, ready and eager to learn his place in the pack. Your dog is coming into a new environment with new rules and a new setup. And you're beginning a new relationship. This means more work now, but it will pay dividends later by making your life – and your new dog's – much easier. Like I've said numerous times so far, start small and slow. Do things incrementally and build on the success you see. It's better to say, "Oh, we could have done that even sooner than we did" than it is to say, "Yikes! We should have waited on that." This includes scenarios like introducing him to other dogs, extending his boundaries, taking on too much too fast, etc. Let him earn his freedom little by little. It's better to give him restrictions in the beginning and loosen them up over time than to give him the run of the house then try to rein him in later.

Get to know your new dog, observe him in various situations, watch his body language and reactions. This will help tune you into his triggers and temperament. Remember, before you had him, he was part of another dynamic and structure. Take into consideration his puppy imprinting — the environment that molded him for his first 8-10 weeks. He had a role within his litter — maybe he was the dominant puppy. Perhaps he was the runt. If you don't know your dog's backstory, just understand he has one. Figure out his drive and what behaviors are rooted in nature and which ones can be modified through nurture.

I highly suggest, for the first two weeks, leaving the leash on when you're home. This gives you more control over him. When you're not home, take the leash off. You don't want to come home and find him tangled around a precariously dangling fish tank. Also keep in mind, there's both nature and nurture at play. Nurture him, build your relationship and foundation, but also realize there are certain parts of him you'll just have to accept and love.

Bringing a new dog home can be a stressful time for everyone involved. This is a huge transition period, especially for the dog, who's trying to learn his role in the family and understand what you expect of him. The key to success is creating the right environment and relationship from the outset — especially during the first two weeks. This is an important period when the dog will really need to be introduced to the rules, structure, routine, and family dynamic. It is also the easiest time to instill these rules, as the dog possesses no pre-existing association to your home — new house, new rules.

Building a solid foundation is the key to success (see training chapter). Start off by implementing a firm structure—this includes crate training, keeping the leash on him in the house and, monitoring him closely when he's roaming freely. As your new dog begins to understand the rules, you can then start to add more freedom, it is far easier on both parties to add privileges as you go along than it is to start off too big and then take away liberties. The premise of this is for your new puppy or adult dog to earn his freedom by meeting the expectations you set for him. Dogs are opportunistic and given the chance, they will take advantage of any perceived weaknesses. You will then have to work that much harder to rein in bad habits that already have become learned behavior during that initial couple weeks.

Remember, ambiguity breeds confusion which equals unwanted behavior. Be consistent and stick to your structure and routine. This will allow your new dog to feel comfortable and secure knowing what is expected of him. It is also important to start off by creating the environment that will be the long-term, What I mean by this is, don't allow the puppy on the couch one day then expect to easily end this behavior when he becomes a full-grown dog. Don't take a week off work, spend all day, everyday with your new dog then suddenly return to work, leaving him for hours at a time. Don't feel sorry for your new rescue dog and all he's been through, consequently spending the first few days with him locked in one continuous hug.

It is also important not to set him up to fail. If you are unsure about housebreaking, don't let him out of your site. If you are unsure about his sociability, don't go to the dog park. Remember, take things slowly and add in extras as you get to know him and he gets to know you. And with consistency and calm leadership, continuously work to build a solid relationship where you and your dog are truly dialed in with one another.

It's very common for people to compare a new dog to the last one they had – for both good and bad. Don't do this. This new dog is a new beginning. He's a completely new dog and you two will build a unique relationship all your own. Allow this to happen without trying to pigeonhole him into the role you want him. Get to know him, allow him to be himself, and tackle his individual issues and bugaboos with a fresh approach custom made for him.

CHAPTER 7

Management

By management, I mean, how will you handle your dog once you're out of training mode? If you think of training as setting up the structure, the management is the routine, or implementation of said structure. Having a happy, healthy dog and enjoying a mutually beneficial relationship with him is a journey, not a destination. It's an ongoing process that you must continually foster and nurture. Many things in life require ongoing maintenance to ensure they continue to work properly – having a dog is one of them.

The main aspect of management is understanding your dog – the good, the bad and the ugly. While many of his bad habits and tendencies can be corrected through training, there are some behaviors that are simply there for the long haul. It is crucial that you fully understand and recognize your dog's dislikes, limitations and stress triggers. Just like with people, each dog is different. Just because you are outgoing and enjoy being surrounded by people, it doesn't mean your dog will as well – and trying to train him to be so will most likely prove futile and frustrating. Sure, you may enjoy a day at the park and find it fun and relaxing, but to your dog is may be stressful and overwhelming, causing him to act out.

Once you have placed your dog in a stressful environment, it will be difficult to get him to listen to you. Dogs must be in a "training state of mind" in order to learn, process and absorb commands and expectations.

The key is to work with your dog first in an environment with little stress and stimulation. As he improves in this type of setting, you may then gradually move his training to higher stimulation areas. As you begin giving him new tools with which to deal with stress, you can then start exposing him to different environments. Due to his new tools and ability to deal with triggers, he will have a new association.

However, if you continue exposing him to his stressors without managing his ability to deal with them, then all that's occurring is he's continuously practicing negative behavior. And as I've said numerous times, practice makes perfect for both good and bad.

While it is true that dogs live in the present, forever focused on the now, some people say that the past is irrelevant. Sure, dogs do not hang on to past experiences like we do, but their past does affect the present and helps shape their associations to various objects, environments and situations. Many owners have a tendency to baby their dogs – especially those they've adopted from a rescue. They believe they must smother him in love in order to make up for his rough past; however, this is as counterproductive as it comes. Your dog's past should be kept in mind but not used as a reason to turn your dog into a needy fearful little brat.

Sadie is one of my all-time favorite dogs. I trained her right after she was adopted and still, to this day, she stays at my house when her parents are out of town. Sadie's life began about a horribly as you can imagine. She was used as a bait dog. Just one look at her scarred face and torn ears tells the story of her early years. She was abused, neglected, exploited and treated as cruelly as it gets by people. However, despite all this, I've literally never met a sweeter, more affectionate and more trusting dog. She doesn't let her past keep her down. With that said, however, she does have trust issues with other dogs. Maybe it's because of her past or perhaps it's just a nature overpowering nurture scenario.

Her parents, however, do have to manage her issues. As I said, she's not dog social, so they take this into consideration. She doesn't go to dog parks, her parents stay hyper-vigilant during walks and they only board her with people they trust understand her limitations. Sadie's parents pick their battles, working on issues that warrant it and accommodating those that don't.

Always keep in mind your dog's limitations – don't put him in situations you know will cause him stress. What drives your dog? Manage around this. If he has strong Pack Drive, tap into this whenever a situation gets tricky. Understand what motivates your dog, what you can do to control any given situation. Choose the path of least resistance, learn from your mistakes and repeat techniques that garner results.

So often, owners come to me hoping I'll train their dog to do certain things. Very often, these are things the owners think the dogs should want to do. For instance, sociability is a big one. Many owners think their dog should want to play with other dogs, romp at the dog park, and make doggie friends. But certain dogs do not enjoy this – and actively dislike it. Don't try to fit a square peg into a round hole. Bubba was a mastiff I worked with whose dad loved going to his local coffee shop.

"Can you make Bubba stop growling at people who walk by our table?" he asked during our session.

"Have you ever considered that Bubba just doesn't like that environment? That it causes him anxiety to have people bobbing and weaving all around him?" I countered.

Accept your dog for who he is and start from there. To continue strengthening your relationship, once the foundation is firmly laid, go back to certain tasks your dog enjoys doing. Maybe he likes sitting on command for a treat. If so, then do this. Take the path of least resistance whenever you can. This will help build and maintain your relationship while also solidifying your role – something you will likely need to fall back on in the case when a stressful situation pops up.

CHAPTER 8

Bringing Home Baby

Any sort of change in a household, be it good or bad, brings about disruptions and instability for everyone involved – and your dog is no exception. The most common, large-scale family change I see when called in for training sessions is the arrival of a new baby. And it usually plays out the same way; everyone's under-slept, overly stressed and on edge. Fuses are slightly shorter, excitement is palpable, family and friends are constantly in and out of the house, and the dog's caught in the middle—confused, anxious and no longer an only child. His behaviors are simply a result of everything he once knew and understood getting flipped on its head – and often overnight. He no longer understands his role in the family. His routine is altered and there's now this strange little being in the house, with its screaming and crying and hogging all the attention. He has no idea how to respond or react and is simply going off instinct.

More often than not, the overnight aspect of this change creates the biggest problem. If you walk through the front door one day with your bundle of joy and just expect your dog to fall in line immediately, you're rolling the dice. Dogs are adaptable and will gel to new environments, but it falls on your shoulders to communicate to him the new guidelines. The trick is putting these new rules into effect early on. Not only will you lack the time and energy to delve into training your dog with a newborn strapped to your chest, but you will be starting from scratch amid all the new chaos

– increasing the amount of stress for everyone. And whether you think this is true or not, no matter how much you adore your dog and swear nothing between you will change once the baby arrives, it's just not realistic. As the environment changes so does the dynamic. And from there, the relationship will also be affected. Sure, your love for him won't diminish, but I guarantee the first time there's a negative interaction between him and your baby, he will shoulder the blame.

For the sake of everyone's sanity, let's prevent this; devise a plan and begin implementing it as early as possible. Is there a room that will become off limits? If so, make it off-limits before the baby comes. Management is key. Remember, the Structure is what you set up and the Routine is the implementation of that structure. So start setting up and implementing the minute that strip turns blue. The reality is, your priorities will change and that's perfectly OK. The key is to maintain balance and happiness throughout this shift. As your family grows and your number of spare hours in the day dwindles, it's important to be more on point with your dog. Your words and interactions become more meaningful. You will no longer have time to spend repeating yourself, so go ahead and start strengthening the relationship between you and your dog ahead of time. This will increase your credibility with him and save you time and headaches down the road.

Because he's a dog and you cannot simply post a revised chore schedule on the refrigerator for him, you need to be proactive. Will there be new boundaries? For instance, will the couch be off limits once baby arrives? If so, communicate this to him from the outset. Do you plan on walking him with the baby in a stroller? Begin practicing this as soon as you purchase it. There's a chance the pram will stress him out – many dogs are frightened by them. With enough time, you can either get him used to it or make adjustments to your plan. Will his routine change? Do you plan on feeding him at different times or in a different location? If so, begin this as soon as possible. This way, by the time baby arrives, these will no longer be changes – they'll simply be his routine. Preparation is key, along with a solid foundation. The important factor is time – giving him enough advance notice of the storm brewin' in your belly.

First, do a maintenance check. Honestly and objectively observe your dog, taking in any bad behaviors you may have let slide. Before baby, these behaviors may seem fairly inconsequential. Sure, he jumps a little and shows a wee bit of possessiveness towards you, but it's really not a big deal. Now consider these behaviors with a baby in the house, in your arms, on your lap. It's important to rope in these issues while the stakes are still low. Revisit the steps to forming a strong foundation. Go back to basics and rein in any and all undesired behaviors. Not only does this provide an opportunity for a training tune-up, it also serves to strengthen your relationship. Many couples take a Babymoon as a way to reconnect and rejuvenate their relationship before becoming parents. Think of this time with your dog in the same way. Make sure you're dialed in with one another, speaking the same language and make repairs as needed — and before you're crazed from sleep deprivation.

Focus on steeling his "Down-Stay" and "Place Mat" commands, as these will be helpful tools to use if and when over-excitement and over-stimulation take over and cause him to react on instinct. Consider all the changes you're making to the house for the arrival of your baby – painting, new furniture, rearranging the layout of certain rooms, making things vomit and pee-resistant. Why wouldn't your dog be included? He's part of the family and his life will inevitably change from the new addition. So, it only makes sense to prepare him, as well. There's also a strong chance your dog will become stressed out or begin behaving differently far before the baby comes. They sense these things – like when you're packing for a trip and he picks up on it and begins trying to sneak into your suitcase.

As you receive baby gifts, buy supplies, furniture and clothing, and prepare a nursery, introduce your dog to all these new items. Let him familiarize himself with the new smells and sights as you go. Gradual, incremental change works best for dogs, and considering you have nine or so months to get ready, it's a perfect opportunity to communicate on his level – to ease him in. Actively include him in the process.

Ok, now that we've covered the pre-baby preparation, let's discuss a few tips for after the baby's arrival. First off, if you've spent the previous few months reinforcing your dog's foundation training, this is the time to put that into use. Use your essential commands to correct unwanted behaviors – such as jumping on you while you're holding the baby or hopping on the couch during feeding time. Just because you've laid down the law ahead of time, that doesn't mean he's not going to try to test the boundaries. He should see the baby as an extension of you, your possession. When you lean down and pull food out of the oven, does he lunge up and grab it? Probably not. And this isn't from a lack of wanting to – it's because he knows that food is yours. Your baby is that Thanksgiving turkey and your dog should understand this. The baby is your new toy, not his.

This should go without saying, but you'd be surprised how often I find myself saying it, but your dog and your baby should never be left together unattended. This is true for many years to come. There are simply too many variables at play that could result in a bad interaction. Allocate both the dog and baby an area that's just theirs – where the other can't go. We all deserve a little personal space. Even if it's just a place mat, make that your dog's and his alone. As your baby gets older, let him have a room or area where he can play and wobble around without your dog interrupting – or inadvertently knocking him over.

Be cognizant of triggers that cause stress in your dog. Stress and anxiety can lead to unwanted instinctive behaviors and should be quelled as quickly as possible. You all may be a little tired and cranky, but unlike you and your spouse, your dog can't simply yell it out or swig a glass of wine when nobody's looking. Remove your dog from stressful situations. If a crying baby triggers anxiety, put him in his crate in another room, cover it with a sheet and let him zone out with a bone. His crate will serve as his go-to place where he can relax and escape the stress. This also communicates to him your expectations at that moment. You're letting him know you don't need his help to quiet the baby, so he can just take it easy. If you're unsure whether or not a specific situation is causing him stress, read his body language. He'll let you know.

I always emphasize the importance of setting everybody up to succeed. This means, don't push it. Take it slow and steady. Don't force situations for the sake of it. Introduce your dog and baby gradually, in small doses, and in a calm environment. The moment the energy changes and chaos ensues, give the dog an escape plan. Let him be himself and warm up to the baby in his own time and in his own way. And among all the changes and restrictions, try not to reduce his exercise; make that the one thing that remains consistent.

So many owners I work with truly consider their dog as part of the family, but somehow forget to fill him in when big, life-altering changes are afoot. This ultimately leads to miscommunication, frustration, and stress for all parties. The good news is, it's easy to prevent so long as you put in a little time, forethought, and effort.

CHAPTER 9

Aggression, It's No Joke

I worked with a young guy a few years back who was in his mid-20s. He and his shepherd/pit mix were the best of friends. Duke was his ultimate sidekick. Among many things, he and Duke used to rough house – a lot. They'd play tug-of-war, wrestle, and even box. That's right, he'd put boxing gloves on Duke and they'd go at it. As the expression goes, "It's all fun and games until somebody gets hurt." In this case, the person who got hurt was a complete stranger Duke bit one day after getting free from his leash. I didn't have the heart to tell the guy he had it coming. After all, he'd taught Duke how these behaviors through overly aggressive play.

When embarking on aggression issues, we must once again ask ourselves those ever-important questions: How are my actions, what I allow, and the environment I provide affecting my dog's behavior? Do I have him set up for success? What could I, as his leader, be doing differently to help reduce his exposure to triggers? And when he is triggered, how am I reacting?

As we've previously discussed, there are generally two approaches in the dog-training world when it comes to changing unwanted behaviors – correction and redirection. To refresh, correction is a punitive action while redirection falls more into the category of positive training methods. So which works better? Well, it is not that simple, especially when it comes to aggression. To take sides and rule out worth from either methodology would be a big mistake.

When teaching our dogs commands like Sit, Stay, and Come, using a reward system is invaluable, like reinforcing his behavior with a treat. This same technique also works when trying to redirect your dog. It allows you to shift his focus off a trigger and onto something more tempting, like a treat.

However, this method is not so effective when aggression is at play. When your dog is exhibiting aggressive behaviors, his body has taken over – the stress and anxiety he feels are at their highest and he is lashing out, looking for that release we discussed in Chapter Three. Most likely, when dealing with aggression, simply redirecting his attention with a treat will not override the physical reaction he is experiencing.

Correction, on the other hand, doles out a consequence to your dog's behavior. Because your dog forms strong associations, he'll begin to learn that certain behaviors lead to unwanted results. Touch a hot iron once and you'll think twice before touching it again. There is a balance that must be struck when correcting aggressive behaviors. If the physical correction is not executed properly, you run the risk of it becoming part of the cycle. Associations can be a double-edged sword in this regard, so it's important your dog doesn't begin associating specific corrections with specific stress and aggression-inducing situations – otherwise, the correction itself could become a trigger.

If this happens, we must use a different form of correction, rebooting his association, so to speak. My own dog, Duchess, constantly evolves and changes, forcing me to switch up my forms of correction regularly. One method will work for a bit, maybe a couple weeks, then it will either become a trigger or Duchess will suddenly be impervious to it. Working with dogs who have aggressive tendencies is an ongoing process, one that requires consistent maintenance checks and adjustments. So if you find yourself in a situation like this – where your current trick or technique is no longer working for whatever reason – then, onward and upward, until you find what works. But always start with the path of least resistance, the methods and tools that are most likely to work.

If we go back to nature and study animals that live in packs, we see that structure and balance are kept by a hierarchy, sometimes reinforced by a higher ranking animal punishing a lower-ranking animal's unwanted behavior in order to keep the peace and ensure survival. Ultimately, it all boils down to survival. Let's face it—did any of us grow up without being punished for unwanted behavior? "Wait until your father gets home" sure made me think twice. However, as we pointed out in Chapter One, dogs don't live in packs of 50, roaming the woods and hunting together. But they do live in a pack of sorts, they are members of our family. And our neighborhoods are the wild, our homes their den and we must fill the role of pack leader.

We first need to accept that aggression is a form of communication, a part of being an animal and a part of life. It's simply part of being a dog. The trick is to communicate to your dog what level of aggression is acceptable versus when he's taken it too far. With the right attitude, approach, and foundation, you will rarely have to punish your dog and he will know what is expected and comply happily.

Because you want to correct his thoughts before they manifest into actions, it's important to always have a read on your dog's mindset. By watching for these aggressive body language signs and using the Aggression Scale, you can stay one step ahead in any situation.

Aggressive Body Language

When dealing with aggression, body language plays a key role. You'll need to learn to read & understand what your dog is telling you through subtle changes in his stance, posture, and even his facial expressions. To accomplish this, you will need to be fully tuned in to your dog, but once you learn his tendencies, he'll be as easy to read as an open book. These indicators vary in their message from, "I'm feelin' feisty" to "It's on!"

Watch For:

- Stiffened body
- Ears back
- Frowning
- Clenched Jaw
- Stiff, high tail
- Puffed-out chest
- Acting Large
- Fur mohawked down the back
- Showing teeth
- Growling
- Cold, hard stare

Aggression Scale

0-2 I'm sleeping or lying down, completely relaxed.

3-4 I may be sitting or standing, I'm alert but not taking action. I'm aware of my surroundings but nothing is triggering me.

5-6 I'm starting to show signs of excitement. I may be pulling on the leash slightly, pacing around the house. I'm on guard, something has caught my attention. This is a good time to apply redirection if you anticipate an increase. They're showing signs of over-stimulation, but they're not completely distracted and in the zone yet.

7-8 I'm amped. I may be lunging a bit harder, growling or starting to bark. I will be harder to redirect at this point, unless I have a strong

Pack Drive. However, if my Prey and/or Defensive Drive is stronger, it might be time to just remove me from this situation.

9-10 I'm completely in the zone. Just remove me from this situation…NOW!

How to Tackle Aggression Issues

Drive also plays a big role in aggression. In fact, it may be the root cause. Pinpointing your dog's drive – be it Prey, Pack or Defensive – is the first step to combating these behaviors. As I said in Chapter 4, understanding what makes your dog tick and motivates him to act in a particular way is the ultimate decoder ring to unlocking his mind. This knowledge will give you foresight and the ability to anticipate his behavior in any given environment. Using the SHARK Effect, you can then turn this knowledge into results. Understand, anticipate and then take small steps to remedy the issue. Take it one day, one walk, one new person or dog at a time. Avoid situations that may trigger his Drive then begin to slowly change his association to these triggers.

Refer back to Chapter 4 to refresh yourself if need be, but here's a quick rundown of the drives.

Prey: Prey aggression is at play when your dog sees a prey-like animal – a squirrel, cat or even a smaller dog – and his instinct to chase, retrieve, or possibly even kill kicks in.

Pack: Think of pack aggression as mob mentality. This behavior is often seen at dog parks or dog daycare, any time there's a pack environment. Dogs, like people, are vulnerable to the Monkey See, Monkey Do tendency.

Defensive: Defensive Aggression occurs when your dog's survival instincts are triggered, causing a physical reaction – fight or flight. While some dogs flee, others choose to fight.

When attempting to alter any behavior, it's best to start slowly; make small changes day-by-day that will compound over time and lead to big results. Let's say you decided to train for your first-ever marathon. Chances are, you wouldn't set out to run 26.2 miles on Day 1. More likely, you'd begin by huffing and puffing your way through a mile or two, only after bribing, threatening or forcing yourself to lace up your shoes and hit the pavement in the first place. However, as the days and weeks clicked by, you'd notice your stamina increasing as your runs become farther and farther with each passing day. You'd no longer require the mind games and self-imposed guilt trips to get yourself out the door and you'd then realize your daily run had become the same as brushing your teeth – a habit.

Starting slowly is essential when it comes to changing patterns of behavior. If, for example, you'd set out on Day 1 to run 26.2 miles, the odds are great that you wouldn't complete your goal – or, if you did achieve it, you'd be in so much pain you'd vow never to run again. In other words, biting off more than you can chew from the get-go isn't being ambitious – it's setting yourself up for failure. The same is true when it comes to your dog. Rome wasn't built in a day and likewise, your dog's undesirable behaviors cannot be remedied that quickly either.

When dealing with an aggressive dog – whether he's aggressive towards people, other dogs or only circumstantially – it's important to take things slow and always set your pup up for success. For example, if your dog acts aggressively towards his own kind, don't toss him into a dog park as a means of desensitizing him – exposure therapy doesn't work with canines! This strategy will only serve to discourage you and cause your dog unnecessary stress – which often exacerbates the issues and is potentially dangerous.

Determine where your dog is most prone to aggression. Does he aggressively protect your front door? If so, this is because he thinks he owns it. Take that territory away from him. Stand in between him and the front door when he begins acting up. Physically walk him away from it — taking steps towards him until he submits. Sitting is usually a sign of submission in this case. If his aggression comes out on walks when he sees a squirrel, get in between him and the object of his desire and again, physically step into him until he backs off. You're providing a physical barrier which will help to reset his state of mind.

Stress, excitement, and over-stimulation are the main root causes of unwanted behavior in dogs – whether it's separation anxiety, destructiveness, aggression and so on. Determining the trigger of your dog's aggression and removing it from the equation will immediately create a calmer environment and put your dog in the right frame of mind to begin deconstructing his bad behavior.

Leash Aggression

Leash Aggression is probably one of the most common complaints I hear when working with owners. You're outside on a walk, there's stimuli all over the place, a plethora of potential distractions, and countless unknown variables that you, as the owner and handler, cannot control. Your dog is not only excited to be on a walk, but he's also overjoyed by all the sights, smells, and sounds – to say he can become overstimulated is an understatement. These factors can create a slippery slope where fun quickly leads into aggression.

Maya was a sweet dog I trained who loved nothing more than running around at the dog park and visiting her friends at dog daycare. She was incredibly social – until the leash appeared. Once she was leashed up for a walk, Maya became a different, aggressive dog. The leash is actually the culprit in this case. It made her feel harnessed back and restricted. Not only that, but the leash was connected to her person which only compounded the issue, causing Maya to switch into Defensive mode. By improving Maya's training foundation inside, where she wasn't distracted and triggered, I was able to help her parents increase their credibility with her. By using the leash inside, we were also able to change her association.

By working on the fundamentals, Maya's parents began to earn her respect and gain more credibility, which they could then utilize on walks. Keeping her dialed in to them with frequent eye contact also allowed them to gauge her state of mind. This in turn provided them the ability to correct her thoughts before she acted. By tapping into Maya's Pack Drive, her parents were able to lead while keeping her focused on them, rather than triggers.

When it comes to leash aggression, you're dealing with a specific entity that's triggering your dog's Prey Drive – a person on a skateboard, a dog across the street, a squirrel in a tree. And when it comes to tackling this behavior, you're going to want to switch him from Prey to Pack Drive at the right time. Timing is key. You don't want to wait until he's acted on his physical response. Rather, you want to correct or redirect the thought – before the action has even occurred. In order to do this, you must first be aware of your dog's triggers, what could set him off and result in aggression. As you're walking your dog, be aware of his body language. Look for signs of stress, fear, over-stimulation, or any other aggression-inducing signals.

For example, if you're walking down the street and see another dog approaching, assuming yours has dog issues, watch for signs like frowning of puffing up of his chest. Once you see these, it's time to redirect his thought. Give the leash a pop, for instance, and say, assertively, "Come!" Have a treat ready as this will not only reinforce his good behavior, but it will also serve to further refocus his attention. Other options would be to make him sit, put him in a down-stay, or even turn and walk the other direction – out of sight, out of mind.

There will be an element of trial-and-error as you test different approaches until finding one that works for your dog. One client I worked with strapped a backpack on his dog, as this gave him a sense of purpose

– like he had a mission to accomplish. When they approached a trigger, the client would speed up their pace into a jog. This made the dog feel as though he was working and kept his mind off the trigger.

For other dogs jogging only serves to rile them up more, as they're already in a heightened state of activity. For these dogs It might work better to completely stop, put them into a relaxing position, like down-stay, and have them give eye contact – focusing all their attention on you while the trigger passes.

Finding what works best for your dog may be a process. Start with the path of least resistance then go from there.

When tackling leash aggression:

- Know your dog's triggers
- Try different methods to see what works best for your dog – which type of redirection is most effective?
- What level of assertiveness works most effectively for your dog?
- What tools work best for your dog? For more vehement and strong dogs, maybe a prong collar is the way to go. Some of you may prefer using a Halti, as it allows you to redirect your dog's entire head.

Dog-On-Dog Aggression in the Home

Dogs typically fall into one of four categories:

- **Dog Social:** These dogs will seek out others to play with and enjoy the pack mentality associated with it.
- **Dog Tolerant:** This type of dog may not seek out play but will engage while also choosing sometimes to 'sit this one out.'
- **Dog Selective:** (*most bully breeds):* These dogs are fine with some but not all and often prefer those of the opposite sex. NOT A DOG-PARK DOG.

- **Dog Aggressive:** NEVER DOG PARKS. An *aggressive dog* will generally take all dogs as a challenge and are always willing to fight. It is possible for these dogs to live with another dog if they are properly trained to build up trust. The owner of an *aggressive dog* must be very structured and experienced, maintaining the right environment. This means *never* leaving the dogs alone together, and never having toys or bones around as this may cause a fight.

As I've mentioned – numerous times – trust is a key issue for dogs. They need to trust one another in order to get along. I frequently see cases where two dogs live together, very happily, and get on great. However, problems arise when it comes to meeting new animals.

"But he loves other dogs! Look how close those two are," a parent might say. The key is, those two dogs trust one another, and that's why there are no issues.

When it comes to dog-on-dog aggression in the home, it all boils down to the simple fact that the dogs are duking it out for the Top Dog role. Like two fighters in the ring, they're trying to dominate each other while working out who's faster, stronger, and more agile. With any dog – but especially in those with aggression issues – it's paramount that there be no struggle for this role. After all, you've already established *yourself* as the Top Dog, right? Well, it's time to reinforce your position – by controlling every aspect of your dog's' lives to remind them who the boss truly is.

The first step is to determine the trigger – the catalyst to the aggressive behavior. Many times this type of aggression is a case of resource guarding. Therefore, remove all toys and bones from the situation. Take away anything and everything that could be deemed as a valuable resource from a dog's perspective. I always say that these sorts of items are best suited for single-dog homes — or in a confined area like the crate — and typically cause more problems than they're worth in multi-dog households. You should also know that jealousy and affection can also trigger dog-on-dog aggression. Dogs may become aggressive when competing for your love and affection – turning you into the juicy bone.

Resource guarding can also bleed over into areas of the house, such as the couch, bed or dining table. I call these areas Prime Real Estate – and you want to avoid giving either one a claim over these spots.

When it comes time to feed your dogs, be sure to separate them; give them their own eating areas so neither one feels that his food is threatened. Like toys, bones and the couch, food is another common trigger. It's important that all dogs feel comfortable while they eat – not like they need to protect their food from an impending raid.

Also keep the dogs separated when you're out of the house. Obviously, you're not there to control the situation, put the dogs in their own areas to ensure nothing happens in your absence.

Maintain a calm environment. Keep stimulation and playing to a minimum. In many instances, play fighting is merely a controlled form of aggression. And you know the expression, it's all fun and games until someone gets hurt. Therefore, it doesn't take much for this to escalate into a full-blown fight. It's your job – as the entity in charge – to make sure they know it's your game to start, stop, and control. It's a good idea to stop the game "just because," to remind them who's the boss.

Continue building your foundation with both dogs. Take time to put their leashes on in the house and put them on their designated places.

Practice their basic commands like Sit, Stay and Come. Building your relationship is a continual process that should be consistently reinforced. As your foundation and relationship strengthen, the trust your dogs have in you will continually increase. As this occurs, your dogs will begin to build trust in each other and form a relationship of their own. And this is the key to creating a harmonious and non-aggressive home. Dogs will not blindly follow you simply because you're a human. They will not automatically accept a new dog in their home unless they trust you as their leader and trust the new arrival. Work them together to build their trust in each other. A strong relationship built on trust must be present in order to quiet an anxious dog's tendency towards aggression. Otherwise, they will feel as though they must defend themselves and their territory. The key is to instill in them the knowledge that they're safe and that the territory in question is not theirs to defend – rather, it's yours.

And always remember, some aggression is normal among animals – even our sweet dogs fall victim to instinct once in awhile. It's not so much about ridding your dog of all his aggressive tendencies; it's about communicating to him what level is OK and what level isn't.

Meeting New Dogs

Before starting this process, you must first ensure your rank is established. If your dog doesn't listen to you when he's by himself, how do you expect him to do so when another dog is around? If anything, the new dog will only pose a distraction, so your foundation and relationship must be firmly solidified. Know your dog first – his Drive, the signals he gives through body language and be sure your dog trusts YOU before attempting to get him to trust another dog. Read him and correct his thoughts before they turn into action. Keep it simple and start off slow. Don't introduce anything into the situation that could cause stress – toys, food, treats, etc.

If you're bringing a new dog into the house – be it a friend's dog who will only be over for a few hours or a new, permanent family member – it's important to do introductions – just like we do upon meeting someone new. However, in the dog world, a firm handshake and friendly, "Nice to meet you," are not options. Therefore, we need to give dogs the opportunity to get to know one another in their own way.

It's also important to remember that your dog may not like all other dogs. Not only are there degrees of dog sociability, but even the friendliest pooch out there may run across those he just doesn't like. After all, do you like every single person you've met throughout your life? Of course not! But there is a proper way to let dogs meet one another that will provide the greatest chance of success – even if that merely means the two ignore one another in calm contentment.

Avoid nose-to-nose introductions. The best way to go about it is to take the dogs to a neutral location – avoid an area that one may consider his turf – and simply walk them together, side by side. Keep them moving and don't allow them to become entrenched in a frozen staring contest. Walk them until each dog is trotting along easily and calmly. Keep the leashes loose and free of tension. Dogs can feel tightness in the leash and will interpret this as you being tense. Your energy and attitude directly affects that of your dog – so stay calm and loose. Dogs respond best to even-keeled leadership.

Once they're walking well together, let them feel each other out by sniffing one another's hindquarters. Continue to avoid nose-to-nose interactions.

Maintaining a calm environment, you can then take the dogs to a backyard and drop their leashes, giving them the freedom to get to know one another untethered. Have a spray bottle handy in case behaviors pop up that need to be corrected. Continue to foster calm energy – as I said earlier, play fighting is still a form of fighting – like two boxers sparring in the ring – and can quickly and easily turn into all out aggression.

When you feel it's time to bring the dogs into the house, it's not a bad idea to block off areas with baby gates, giving each dog their own space. This allows them to interact through the gate without either feeling threatened or stressed. Even through a barrier like a baby gate, dogs are still able to get to know one another and become accustomed to the other's presence.

A solid recall is also important. Make sure your dog's "Come" command is solid.

Never leave them alone together and remember, size matters. Two Yorkies getting into a brawl probably won't result in much damage. However, two bullies or a bully and a Yorkie, that's a different story entirely.

I always advise my clients to go slow. It's much better to delay full immersion than to rush it. You'd rather say, "Oh, we could have done that much sooner" than it is to wish you'd waited a bit longer – this will also help to set your dog up for success. Always maintain a calm environment and keep stimulation to a minimum. Over-stimulation and excitement can easily morph into aggression and send the whole process on a backslide. Just remember – you're in control and for the sake of you and your dogs, set the stage for success, not failure.

Transfer Aggression

Transfer aggression occurs when dogs become so frustrated and stressed out they turn on one another or on you. Take two dogs in a backyard, for instance. They're playing and sniffing and going about their business – until someone walks past the fence. Then, all hell breaks loose as they begin barking and jumping at the fence in crazed excitement. But they're unable to get to the person or other dog. Thus, they'll take all that frustrated energy and turn it on each other. This also commonly occurs on walks, when dogs don't have the freedom to run and chase every bird, squirrel or cat that catches their attention.

Ollie and Cleo were two pit mixes I trained a while back. They were the best of buds and got along without a hitch. One day, however, things got messy. Ollie and Cleo were in their backyard, sniffing, sunbathing and relaxing, when out of nowhere gardeners appeared next door. The stress from the leaf blower, lawn mower and weed whacker proved too much for this dynamic duo. The two turned on each other and the entire ordeal ended with blood and stitches.

If this is a behavioral issue you're experiencing, first try to locate the source. Is there something in particular that sets your dogs off and leads to this type of aggression? Perhaps it's passing other people or dogs on the street, folks walking by your yard or even a squirrel darting up a tree that sends your dogs into a tizzy. Though you may not be able to remove or avoid the trigger, it's still good to know what it is so you can be prepared.

Transfer aggression often occurs in certain areas; like the front door or fence line. You see, dogs feel differently in different areas. In the spots where they exhibit transfer aggression, they feel powerful – as if it's their territory. It's important to reclaim this area as yours, thus taking away your dog's power and perceived need to act aggressively.

Never leave dogs with transfer aggression alone together – especially since you cannot necessarily control the trigger in this scenario.

At first, walk your dogs separately. Rather than walking both together for 30 minutes, trying taking each on its own 15-minute walk. This will allow you one-on-one time to really focus on each dog's behavior. Work on controlling each of your pooches and helping them to become comfortable and relaxed on walks. Also, with this method, you will avoid transfer aggression, as the dogs won't have each other to turn against.

Prey Aggression

Prey aggression is fairly self-explanatory. If your dog becomes Cujo-esque at the sight of a squirrel, cat, bird or any type of prey animal, then you're dealing with prey aggression. This issue is fairly difficult to vanquish completely, as it's in a dog's nature to go after prey. However, there are some techniques to help take the edge off.

As we've discussed, the leash exacerbates this issue. It holds your dog back, creating frustration and excitement to build up into a frenzy. The goal in correcting this is to switch your dog from Prey Drive into Pack Drive.

First, a strong recall is essential. You need to know that your dog will come when he's called, as this will be your method of redirecting his attention. Along these same lines, learn your dog's threshold. For instance, perhaps your dog is able to be recalled and redirected 20 feet out from the squirrel. Know his threshold.

Always remain dialed in to your dog's body language. Learn the signs – maybe he begins to lunge or his ears go back. Or perhaps his body simply stiffens subtly. Whatever his tell-tale signs, learn them and stay tuned in on walks.

Then, slowly desensitize him. By this, I mean take your time and extend his threshold. Again, take this very, very slowly. And make sure you're always vigilant of his body language – because once you've reached his threshold, chances are it's GO time!

People Aggression

Dogs that exhibit aggression towards people typically come from a place of fear and lack of trust – i.e. Defensive Drive. This fear creates anxiety that then manifests itself as aggression. While recognizing the cause may help you approach your dog with a bit more understanding, saying, "Don't mind him, he's just scared," offers little consolation as your friends huddled against the front door.

People Aggression often perpetuates itself in a territorial issue I call the Mailman Effect. Meaning, your mailman walks up on your front porch and your dog charges the front door, barking and growling. Then the mailman turns and leaves. While we know this is simply because he's finished delivering the mail, in your dog's mind, he's thinking, "I'm the best guard dog ever! I chased him away." He's gotten the result he wants, thus reinforcing this behavior.

In this situation it's essential to go back and work on the foundation and relationship you've built with your dog. This will ensure he trusts you and is confident and secure in your leadership. This will then allow him to trust you implicitly, in any situation – such as meeting a new person. He'll learn to trust that if you're allowing someone to enter the house or approach you, that must mean they're good people. This then communicates to him that his services aren't needed.

You need to change the association your dog has with a new person. Make that person part of the solution rather than the problem. Give your friend a treat to give your dog, once he's "Come" at your friend's command.

Have your friend take your dog on a walk in order to build trust. Walks on a leash often establish the handler's role as the leader.

This will help desensitize your dog. But remain aware of your dog's threshold and take it slowly.

Start off small and always leave the situation on a positive note. This will help shift his association. The key is to give your dog a longer fuse, but do this gradually. Don't do too much too soon. After your dog eats his treat, remove him and let him relax in his crate. On their second meeting, let them sit together for a bit, then remove him once again. Build it up.

Management is key in these situations – where is your dog most relaxed and comfortable? Where is he most easily triggered? Have a game plan.

For an anxious, fearful dog, eye contact can be threatening. Let new people know this so they can avoid triggering a fear-based reaction.

When bringing guests into the home, it's a good idea to go through a Greeting Routine. It's best to let your dog meet new people in a neutral area – like on the street. This way, he can first get to know them in a space he doesn't feel he must protect.

Once in the house, put him on his leash and send him to his placemat. Once you've gotten him to lie down, bring in your guests. They should ignore him completely – any interaction could be perceived as reinforcement by the dog, so you want to avoid this altogether. Allow your guests and dog to simply be in the room together, giving your pooch time to become used to their presence.

Give him the command to Sit and make sure he's giving you eye contact. Then give him a treat and instruct him to Stay. Keep his leash in your hand – still making him stay – and walk over to the new person. Let them take a treat and show it to the dog. Have the person then call your dog over to receive the treat. This way, your dog associates this stranger with something positive – food!

If your pooch continues to exhibit signs of aggression, call him to you and then have the new person call him to them. Do this as many times as needed, depending on the severity of the aggressive behavior.

If after one time back and forth your dog seems to become more comfortable, have the new person take the leash and walk your dog. This will help to assert that new person's leadership. However, if the person is fearful, this will translate as untrustworthy to your dog – so only allow them to walk your dog if they're giving off calm and assertive energy.

Once your dog has remained calm around your guests for five minutes, take him to a different room and place him in his crate.

It's very important, when rewarding your dog, that you reward his thoughts – not his actions. This is where body language is extremely useful. If your dog's body is stiff and he's staring down your friend, don't give him a treat simply because he's not on top of your guest. His body language will communicate to you where his thoughts lie – and those are what must be rewarded and corrected.

Remember to always leave things on a positive note and not to overdo it or push the envelope. Take it slowly.

Food Aggression

When it comes to food and your dog, he needs to earn it. Not own it. Make him work for his dinner, as this will remind him who's in charge.

Don't place your dog's food in a corner – this forces him to eat with his back turned towards the room, which will increase his defensiveness. Place his bowl in the middle of his eating area.

Hand feed him at first, making him earn each bite by following your commands. Keeping his leash on, give him a bite or two of food then recall him back to you. When he obeys, give him more food. This will change the dog's association to his food. Rather than being a meal he scarfs down, it has now become part of his training.

Toys

The truth of the matter is some dogs just shouldn't have toys – it's as simple as that. They hold too much value and possess far too much meaning to some. Toys just aren't always worth the trouble. Toy aggression typically shows itself when you try to take a toy from your dog's mouth. For some, the dog growls, runs away to hide, or even snaps, but there is a way to change your dog's association and decrease this reaction.

Using a high value treat – something you know your dog really likes and will motivate him to work harder – hold the toy in your hand. Make sure your dog's leash is on, stand on it so the dog cannot run away. Replace the toy with the treat. This will teach him that when he gives up his favorite ball, he'll get something in return.

If there is a particular toy that brings out the absolute worst in your dog – as in, he won't even let you take it from him – then it is simply too meaningful to him. It possesses far too much value and should be removed from the equation or just thrown away altogether.

Protectiveness

Protectiveness is rooted in Defensive Drive and it all boils down to credibility and trust. If your dog trusts you, he won't feel the need to protect you.

Most likely, your protective dog isn't actually protecting you from anything. He simply becomes aggressive because he thinks you need protecting – perhaps it's time to practice your calm, assertive leadership skills. In this situation, the first step is to recognize what's triggering this reaction. Then, you must convey to your dog that you are in control and do not need his protection. By going back and working on the foundation and relationship, you can say to your dog – in his own language – "Hey, I got this! I'm in control and don't need protection. I'll protect you so you can just go on and relax!"

Each of these solutions is geared towards changing the dog's association with whatever triggers his aggression. This will allow him to build a different perception of that person, place or thing and no longer feel the need to take charge of the situation. It also all circles back around to the foundation and relationship you've built with your pet. These serve as the building blocks on which your dog's trust in you grows. The key is to help him understand that you have matters under control and he no longer needs to be fearful and therefore act aggressively. A dog that is confident in its leader and secure in its environment has nothing to fear and thus, no reason to lash out in aggression. Without the proper relationship and level of trust, no amount of tricks and tips will truly remedy the problem at its root.

Like with transfer aggression, your dog feels powerful over whatever area he's protecting. Reclaim it as yours. Let him know you have things under control and that you're protecting that area. You, or another person in your house, can also become the source of his protectiveness; his possession, his juicy bone. Be sure not to enable this or perpetuate it. When his demands to be on your lap seem less than affectionate and bordering on possessiveness, don't allow it. Again, it goes back to communicating to him his role and reminding him that you're the boss.

In conclusion, the last thing I want to really hit home is this – always take it slow and make sure you're setting everyone up for success. The key is to gradually change your dog's association to whatever trigger is provoking his aggression. By understanding the cause – food, fear, a sense of protectiveness, etc. – and combining this knowledge with the right attitude and tools, you will be better equipped to tackle his aggression issues head-on. This may require you to make a change in how you're approaching things – be it the tools you're using, how you handle your dog, your routine, what you expose him to or even the setup of your home. But changes like these are a small price to pay for the significant, life-enhancing improvements you'll see in your dog. After all, do you want to spend his entire lifetime correcting him? Of course not – our goal is for these new, desirable behaviors to become the norm – that way, you can focus on enjoying every interaction, experience and day you share with him.

CONCLUSION

Rover and Out

The dog-human bond is about as special as it gets. But like any close relationship in your life, it will have its ups and downs. It's moments of sheer bliss mixed with times for reassessing and tweaking. There will be days you can't get enough of each other and instances when you can barely stand the sight of one another. It's a journey, not a destination. Like with anyone you're close to and interact with on a constant basis – be it a spouse, significant other, relative or best friend – the relationship you have with your dog is dynamic. It's constantly evolving based on circumstances, life events and even daily mood swings. Simply reading this book and laying the training foundation are great and important steps in the right direction, but don't stop there. Continue working with your dog in order to establish these newfound good behaviors as habits. Apply the SHARK Effect whenever possible. As life throws curve balls, don't simply duck out of their way. Find simple steps you can take to make them less challenging and overwhelming. At the end of the day, you and your dog are meant to bring one another joy and companionship, not frustration and confusion.

Learning to reach your dog on his level is not only a helpful tool for maintaining harmony, but it's also rewarding and enjoyable. Understanding what makes him tick in any given situation, unraveling his quirks and reactions, and figuring out his unique little personality on a deeper level make up some of the most fun aspects of a relationship. Once you embrace and understand who he is, you can then find the most effective ways to reach him on his level. Through his body language, you'll be able to tell what he's thinking even before he acts, allowing you time to take the appropriate action. Knowing what drives him will provide you with a sixth sense, of sorts, and knowledge regarding what situations could prove more challenging and how to maintain control. You'll also discover what you can do to get the most out of him – what your tone and body language convey, how your reactions either quell or exacerbate situations, and ways in which you can further earn his trust and respect in order to become an even stronger leader. The mixed signals will gradually vanish and lines of communication open up, allowing you and your dog to simply enjoy a healthy, balanced relationship. Until one day, when you look up and realize the two of you are on the same page, with neither of you having to wonder, "What'd you do that for?"

SUMMARY

Memory Joggers

Your dog is a living, breathing, sniffing, feeling, and evolving being. Like us, our dogs change over time. One day he may love his dog food then hate it the next. We've all been there; scouring the shelves at Petco, buying brand after brand hoping to find one he'll actually eat. Their likes and dislikes evolve and so must we. Thus, dog training can't be seen as a one-stop shop to fixing your dog. It's not like a broken bone, where your doctor sets it, puts it in a cast and then six weeks later you're good to go. Reading this book once and implementing all the various techniques, tools and words of wisdom is a great start, but there's a chance that six months from now you may need to refer back to refresh your memory. Or maybe a new issue pops up in a year after a big life change — for instance, you break up with your boyfriend, he moves out, and then suddenly you find yourself being awakened by your dog peeing on you at 2 in the morning, several nights in a row. And yes, that actually happened to an owner I worked with a few years ago.

The bottom line is, life doesn't stand still — it's constantly bobbing and weaving, ebbing and flowing, shifting and changing — taking you and your dog along for the ride. So, when a curve ball comes flying at you and your dog suddenly starts pooping in your closet or nipping at the neighbor, don't get frustrated and overwhelmed. Remember, there's a reason. And while I'd love you to think you'd pick up this book and joyfully read it again, cover-to-cover, I realize that may not be realistic. So here are some reference points to jog your memory if or when your dog starts peeing on you in bed.

- **Communication is Key:** Through your body language, tone, energy and actions, what message are you conveying? Do they all line up or are you sending mixed signals? Ambiguity breeds confusion, so be clear in what you're saying and how you're saying it.
- **Credibility:** Do you have it? When you give a command, do you follow through or let it slide?
- **Trust & Respect:** These are the two most important components — if you don't have your dog's trust and respect, then you don't have credibility as his leader. And you earn these through calm, assertive and consistent leadership.
- **There's a New Sheriff in Town:** Through his unwanted behaviors, your dog has taken over. It's time to let him know you're in charge. You're the leader, you've got things covered. But you must back this up and have credibility in order for him to believe you.
- **Root Causes vs. Symptoms:** Bad behaviors like biting, jumping, peeing in the house and lunging on the leash are symptoms stemming from a root cause — like fear, anxiety, insecurity, nature, drive, etc. Treat the cause, not just the symptom. And recognize and accommodate your dog's natural predisposition and limitations.
- **Know Your Dog:** In any given situation, your dog is communicating with you through his body language. Learn his language — what are his triggers? What environments and situations trigger what reactions? What is his drive?
- **Understand the Family Dynamic:** Your dog is part of your family, so what's his role? Don't tell me, tell him! Make sure he knows what's expected of him.
- **It's a Relationship:** You and your dog have a relationship, just like you do with your spouse, partner, mom or child. Nurture it. And

like with other people in your life, don't ask your dog to be something he isn't. Communicate to him what you want and need from the relationship in a way he understands. Then accept him for who he is.

- **Be Self-Aware:** Be conscious of how you contribute to your dog's behavior — which of your actions cause which of his reactions. Are you unwittingly reinforcing bad behavior by rewarding him when he's in the wrong state of mind?
- **Know Your Stuff:** Truly understand the various training methods and the difference between them — even Pack Training and Pure Positive. While I don't think they are effective on their own, they do have their benefits when used in conjunction with one another and other methods and techniques. Understand the difference between Correction and Redirection — when they should be used, which is more effective for your dog in certain situations, and how to use them.
- **Faux Paws:** We all make mistakes — sometimes we don't even realize it. Understand the various Training Faux Paws. Be honest with yourself — do you fall into one of these categories?
- **Use the Right Tools:** Find the training tool(s) that works best for your dog, his issues and your environment. Start simple — if the easiest tool works, like a spray bottle, then you're set. When it comes to the more serious gear, make sure you buy high quality and use it correctly.
- **Take the Path of Least Resistance:** Rather than banging your head against the wall trying to train your dog not to nip at the cable guy, just put him in his crate. Do you really need him to like the cable guy? Rather than running out to buy E-Collars and expensive equipment to keep your dog from barking at the mailman, first try using a spray bottle. Only increase your effort when it's necessary.

- **Set Everyone Up to Succeed:** Don't take your dog out twice a day then wonder why he's having accidents in the house. Don't take your anti-social dog to the park and wonder why hell breaks loose. Know your dog and use common sense.
- **SHARK Effect:** Learn, understand and implement the SHARK Effect. Take everything step-by-step, day-by-day. Implement simple changes that will gradually become habits — part of your daily routine. It's about making life as easy, happy, and balanced as possible for you and your dog. No issue is too big.
- **Your Dog's Perspective:** How does your dog relate to you and your environment? Be mindful of his perception of his role, your role, where he fits in the family dynamic and what messages he's picking up from you.
- **Your Perspective:** How do you relate to your dog and the way he experiences things? It's a 2-way street. Understanding needs to go both ways.
- **Cause and Effect:** Like with any relationship, how you act affects your dog's behavior. Be mindful of your energy and know that he's tuned into it. If you get excited, he'll follow suit. If you're calm and relaxed, he'll gel to that.
- **Leave Your Baggage at the Door:** Don't put your emotional baggage on your dog. Don't expect him to fill a role in your life that's not in his nature. He's not your therapist or your security blanket or your spouse. He's your dog. It's not his job to fulfill your emotional needs.
- **Expectations:** Keep them realistic — at all times and in all situations.
- **Don't Force a Square Peg into a Round Hole:** Your dog is who he is. Don't try to force him to be something he's not. Behaviors can be altered but his nature and personality cannot.

- **Accept His Limitations:** Just like you, your dog isn't perfect. Don't expect him to be. Know him. Take him as far as you can with training, then accept and accommodate his shortcomings. After all, he doesn't demand perfection from you.
- **Drive:** Understand the various drives. Learn what drives your dog. Remember, he can switch drives very quickly depending on the situation and his personality. Some dogs are only strong in one drive while other can exhibit all of them.
- **Take Control:** Once you've pinpointed your dog's drive(s), take charge. Know what situations will bring it out in him and be ready to correct, redirect or switch him into a different drive. Know how to change it when the need arises.
- **Nature vs. Nurture:** Control and change what you can through nurture, but understand that nature plays a role, as well.
- **Foundation:** Build a strong foundation that you can fall back on when issues arise. Having a solid training foundation will not only help you feel more in control in sticky situations, it will also remind him of the same thing.
- **Boundaries:** During training, use boundaries as a way to practice his Stay command. Put him in a Down-Stay then walk into the kitchen, making the doorway a boundary. This will help reinforce this command and teach him to stay until you release him. In general, give him off-limits areas; the couch, your kid's room, etc. This will help keep him reined in, allow you to keep an eye on him and establish your role as the leader.
- **Affection Through Training:** Training gives you a great opportunity to dole out affection. For starters, your dog's in a good state of mind. Secondly, he's earning the affection and lastly, it helps reinforce his positive behaviors.

- **Structure and Routine:** Implement a structure that's best suited for you, your dog and your environment. Once you've established what works most effectively, make it a routine. Consistency is important.
- **Recognize Triggers:** This goes back to knowing your dog. What triggers his fear, anxiety, tendency to nip? Knowing is half the battle.
- **Tone Matters:** Be matter of fact when you give your dog a command. Don't ask, tell. Don't use a baby voice, that will just excite or confuse him and dilute the command. Be mindful of your tone.
- **Your Body Language:** When telling your dog to sit, don't crouch down in front of him. He'll think you're inviting him in for affection. And conversely, when telling him to come, don't make yourself threatening. Match your body language and tone to the command you're giving.
- **Use Treats:** In the beginning, use treats as a way to reinforce positive behavior. As you work through the foundation commands, they should be used to teach him that when he obeys, he's doing what's expected of him. If you feel your dog is not food/treat motivated, try using them in conjunction with training. Often times, dogs like to earn that reward but show indifference when it's merely handed to them. Gradually wean him off the treats so he's obeying because you say so — not simply to get a juicy morsel.
- **Monkey See, Monkey Do:** I recently worked with a pit bull named Gus. Gus was showing signs of aggression when people entered his house. When his parents called me, they told me all about him and his issues. It wasn't until I showed up for our session that I met Rosie, their four-pound Chihuahua. Within just a few minutes, I realized Rosie was calling the shots. She'd bark and nip at people when they came through the front door, but because of her size, it went unnoticed. In Gus, however, a 70-pound pit, these behaviors are tough to ignore. But he wasn't the root of the problem, he was

just feeding off Rosie's energy. He learned these behaviors from her. Make sure you know which dog is creating the chaos and tackle it at its source. This is also a good example of how different dogs are motivated by different drives.

- **Management:** How are you going to handle your dog once out of training mode? Make a game plan that works for you and your dog. If a potentially stressful situation is on the horizon, how will you deal with it? If one arises out of the blue, still have a game plan ready to execute.
- **Pick Your Battles:** Choose which situations are worth working through and which ones should just be avoided. If he's bad on walks, then that needs to be dealt with; however, if he hates the gardener, just remove him from the yard. Path of least resistance!
- **First Two Weeks:** In the first two weeks of having a dog, set boundaries. This is the time to establish your role, communicate your expectations and show him his place in the family. Start off small and let him earn freedom as time goes on. It's easier to give him fewer liberties then gradually ease up than it is to give him free rein only to harness him back in later.
- **It's Natural:** Aggression is part of nature and part of being a dog. It doesn't mean he's a bad dog or broken. His aggression is a reaction — it's up to you to find another way to channel his thoughts.
- **Correction and Redirection:** These are great tools for combating aggression and managing situations that might cause an aggressive reaction. But you must have a strong relationship with your dog first — for these to work, you need credibility and his trust and respect.
- **His Body Language:** Reading your dog's body language is key in avoiding aggressive reactions. The moment you see his tail stiffen or

his eyes fixate, take action. Don't wait until it's too late to correct or redirect.

- **Thoughts Before Actions:** Once you observe his body language switch to indicate aggression, take control of the situation. Correct his thought before he has the chance to act on it. Remember, dogs think about one thing at a time.
- **Know Your Dog's Threshold:** How close can you get to another dog before he becomes aggressive, anxious, fearful, etc.? Work within this threshold and gradually shorten it as you see positive results. Take it slow. Don't push it and don't do too much too soon.
- **Have Realistic Goals:** Don't expect pigs to fly. You can rein in behaviors and make them more manageable, but you can't change your dog's entire personality and disposition. Not all dogs are social. And while you can get them to a place where they're able to pass another dog on the street without flipping out, he will probably never be a dog park enthusiast.
- **Practice Makes Perfect:** For better and worse. Behaviors your dog practices repeatedly become learned. If every time he begs for food you give him a nibble, he learns that behavior. Then these behaviors become habits. Only practice those you want to become habits.
- **Types of Aggression:** There are different types of aggression. Know which one your dog has and the ways to manage it. Understand why he's acting aggressively in those situations and what instinctually drives him.
- **Association:** The power of association is strong in dogs — both positive and negative. Changing his association to triggers is an important step in dealing with the root cause of an issue.
- **Dogs are Opportunistic:** If you're not a credible, trusted and respected leader, your dog will take that opportunity to push boundaries and attempt to usurp your role. This is also true for the

trash can — if you know your dog raids it every time you leave, then stop leaving it out. Don't give him the opportunity to misbehave or take control of a situation.

- **Be Controlling:** Be controlling so your dog can get on with being cute.

APPENDIX

Coming from a background in dog rescue and often dealing with pit bulls and pit mixes, I feel a moral obligation to take this opportunity and dole out some words of wisdom on these subjects. If you're curious about the ins-and-outs of adopting a dog, keen on learning more about pits or interested in how to responsibly rehome a dog, these following pages will serve you well.

You and Me and Fido Makes Three

If you're at all dialed in to the dog world, I'm sure you've heard the expression "Adopt, Don't Shop" flying around. If you haven't heard those exact words, there's no doubt you're aware of the push towards adopting animals from shelters and rescue groups rather than purchasing cats and dogs from breeders or puppy mill-supplied pet stores. After 10 years of eating, breathing, and living dog rescue, I am obviously a huge proponent of adoption. There are simply too many wonderful animals sitting in shelters at risk of euthanasia for us to be purchasing pets from for-profit establishments. Adopting – or rescuing – in-need animals is an essential ingredient to ending our country's pet overpopulation problems. Not to mention, it's an incredibly rewarding experience, knowing you've truly saved a life.

However, with that said, I know I cannot impose my will and make everyone adopt. Some people will go to breeders regardless of what I, or anyone else, says. For those of you who decide to take the breeder route, please do your homework. Not all breeders are created equally. Just because they have a shiny, nice website, it doesn't mean dogs aren't being bred in truly horrible conditions and irresponsibly. When you begin doing your research, you'll find a wide variety – everything from backyard breeders, just looking to make a quick buck and typically not too concerned with humane and proper breeding practices, to AKC breeders. Be aware, when not done properly, breeding can go very wrong. Many breeders, who are just in it for the money, will over breed their animals. Not only does this cause the mother harm, it also amps up the likelihood of passing along genetic health issues. Also be aware of the misconception that buying a purebred puppy will prevent any bad behavioral issues down the road. Some of the most challenging cases I've had were puppies purchased from breeders – and reputable ones, at that. I'd like to mention a few things before stepping off my soapbox. First, let's dispel the popular myth floating around that dogs from rescue groups and shelters are damaged goods. This is simply not true. All dogs are different. You can find purebred dogs and puppies at both rescues and shelters. Really, I promise. You may have to look a little harder and be patient, but they're there. They each come with their own set of issues, quirks, and personality traits. The key is to find the right fit for you and your lifestyle. It's all about temperament, temperament, temperament. Why are you getting a dog? To have a running partner? A cuddle buddy? Choose a dog whose energy and temperament best fit what you're wanting.

I once worked with a woman and her husband who had bought a Newfoundland — an extra-large, strong and super adorable breed. Both the husband and wife had passive personalities and weren't the most athletic people I'd ever met. When I asked why they got such a powerful breed, they cited his appearance.

"He's just so cute," the husband said. "And as adults, they're very striking dogs."

When I then asked why they got a dog in general, the wife told me they decided it would be a good practice run before having a baby. "We just figured we should try our hand at having a dog before we jump into parenthood," she said, watching as her 50-pound puppy tore through the living room.

Within six months the dog was with new owners and just two short years later, the couple was divorced. I cannot stress enough, avoid choosing a dog based on appearance — temperament is everything.

If you do decide to purchase a dog, make sure you know exactly what you're getting into. Not only do you need to research the specific breeder, you need to really get to know the breed you're interested in. Spend time around them, read everything you can, and take it all into consideration. You must also consider what you will do with the dog if the situation doesn't work out. When adopting from a rescue, you have the opportunity to return the animal back to the safety of the organization. With breeder dogs, you do not typically have this luxury. Be sure to consider all possible circumstances before committing to a dog and buying one.

When it comes to adopting a new family pet, there are two main options. You can either rescue a cat or dog directly from your local shelter or go through a rescue group – it's simply a matter of personal preference depending on your priorities. There are Pros and Cons to each, but at the end of the day, you're giving a homeless pet his second chance.

Just remember – don't try to fit a square peg into a round hole. Just because you love the way beagles look, that doesn't necessarily mean that's the best choice for you. It's all about temperament. Also, before you are seduced by those big eyes and puppy breath, really ask yourself if you want a puppy. They are a real handful and require much more work than a slightly older dog. Plus, with a more mature dog, you have a better gauge of his personality – there's less room for him to surprise you as he grows out of his puppy stage. There are pros and cons to all dogs – and even to having a dog in general. So, do both the dog and yourself a favor, truly weigh them all before acting on this decision.

Animal Shelters

Your local animal shelter is a city or county-run facility that houses dogs, cats, rabbits, hamsters and a whole slew of other animals that no longer have a home. Whether their owners have turned them in, no longer able or willing to care for them, or they were found roaming the streets as strays, pretty much all homeless animals find themselves in a shelter at time or another. Shelters are not the coziest of places due to overcrowding and underfunding. The staff and volunteers typically do the best they can, but there's only so much they can do. At present, some four million or so animals are euthanized in shelters annually. Some of these animals are sick or have extreme behavioral issues, but for the vast majority it comes down to lack of space. Most shelters do not have the room to house all the animals brought to them; thus, space must be made.

Therefore, when you adopt a pet from the shelter, you are undoubtedly saving a life. That animal was in imminent danger of euthanasia. And I can tell you, there is no more rewarding feeling in the world. Another bonus to rescuing an animal directly from the shelter is the adoption process. The fees are generally significantly lower than those at a rescue group and because these facilities are so desperate to place their animals in homes, it's typically fairly quick and easy – very little hassle and fuss. If the pet you've chosen is already spayed or neutered, you'll usually be able to take it home that day. If it isn't, your wait is still only a day or two – then voila, your new family member is ready to head home!

On the downside, however, shelters sometimes prove emotionally taxing for soft-hearted animal lovers. It's difficult to walk among the cages and see all those hopeful eyes staring out through the bars, willing you to pick them. Only picking one can be heart-wrenching when there are so many deserving animals in need. I can tell you from experience, however, the thought of visiting a shelter is usually far worse than the actual experience – more often than not, people leave filled with warm feelings, knowing they're providing a home for a pet that so desperately needs and deserves one.

It's also important to know that shelters animals often have minor medical issues that will need veterinary care; these can range in severity from simply Kennel Cough and eye infections to skin problems and respiratory infections. Once the pet is yours, all subsequent costs are also yours. So while the adoption itself may cost less than at a rescue, follow-up care may stretch your pocketbook a bit.

Lastly, because shelters suffer from overcrowding and a lack of resources, it's very likely you'll receive little information about your new pet in terms of its temperament, sociability and training. The shelters environment causes a great deal of stress on the animals. Therefore, it's difficult for staff to thoroughly assess personality and behavior. There's a good chance that the shy, sweet dog you saw in the shelter will come out of its shell once home. Or, that pup that seemed housebroken at the shelter may have always pottied on the newspaper simply due to its tight living quarters. And, in fact, it may not be potty trained at all. The bottom line, there are no guarantees when rescuing an animal from a shelter – that is, except for the guarantee that you've just saved a life.

Rescue Groups

Rescue groups are nonprofit organizations that take animals out of shelters and place them in new homes. They're essentially the middle men. They do much of the legwork for you in terms of evaluating the animals and pulling out those that they believe are most adoptable. Typically, once sprung from the shelter, a dog then goes to stay with a foster or to a boarding facility. A foster is someone who temporarily houses and takes care of a dog or cat as the search for its new home begins. When you adopt through a rescue group, you are still indirectly saving a life. Though your new dog was not at risk of being euthanized, his spot can now be filled by a pup who is.

Adopting from a rescue is a much more hands-on experience. A good rescue knows a great deal about their dogs. Because of the foster system, a dog's habits, personality, and behavior can be better evaluated in a low-stress home environment. A dog's sociability also can be monitored through adoption fairs and volunteer outings – events where the dogs are taken out and about into the community, giving people the chance to meet (and hopefully fall in love with and adopt) them.

A dog adopted through a rescue will typically come with a clean bill of health, as the organization takes care of medical issues after bailing him from the shelter. You'll also be informed of any pre-existing conditions the dog may have, such as allergies or a susceptibility to ear infections.

In the case you are no longer able to care for your dog, most responsible rescue groups will take back the dog – regardless of how many years have passed since you adopted him. This brings peace of mind, as many owners are forced to make the horrible decision of taking their pet to a shelter in this circumstance. When the pet was in danger of euthanasia when you first adopted it, this option doesn't bode well as the animal is now just an older version of itself. However, once part of a rescue group, a dog is always welcomed back.

There are downsides to going through a rescue group, however. First off, the initial adoption fee is typically between $200-$500. Though this may seem steep, remember that the money is going back into the rescue to enable them to save more dogs. And it's tax deductible. Also, on average, the rescue spends significantly more than this on each dog, as it pays for its vaccinations, spay or neuter, and its living expenses while in the organization's care.

Adopting through a rescue also can be a bit time-consuming, as you must fill out an application and meet all the rescue's requirements – which can be stringent. Not to mention, the rescue holds all the power in determining whether or not you are approved, and being denied is not as rare as you might think. Once the group approves you, they will typically require a home visit – in order to inspect your home and deem it fit for the pet. Once you have your new canine companion at home, don't be surprised if the rescue group contacts you to follow up. It's hard not to wonder how a dog you saved is doing in his new home.

Both routes will provide you with a rewarding and fulfilling experience, as you are saving an animal in need. Just remember, the journey doesn't end once your new dog is home. You saved his life, now it's time to provide him the comfort, security, and contentment he so deserves.

If you do adopt, don't fall into the trap of smothering your new dog with love, assuming he's had an absolutely miserable life and it's now your duty to make up for it. Don't feel sorry for him, otherwise he'll just take over. People often assume any dog with a scar was once a bait dog or that a fearful pup must have been abused. This is not always the case. Let's not conjure up a backstory but rather, deal with the present. Sometimes I work with extremely fearful dogs who've known nothing but love, kindness, and affection. Other times, I see dogs, all scarred up, who are as sweet and well balanced as they come. Don't make up a backstory for your dog then act on it. Get to know your dog for who he is, not what or where he once was.

Really do your research, consider all factors then go from there. Find a dog that fits you, your family, your environment, your lifestyle. If you work long hours, maybe a senior dog is right for you – a mellow little guy who can live out his remaining years in a peaceful and tranquil atmosphere. And again, don't be sucked in by the adorableness of puppies – they really are not right for everyone. A 2-year-old dog may be a better route; they are still young, but require less effort and you already know what you're getting, for the most part.

If you are not fully ready for this commitment – one that can last many, many years – then please do not get a dog. Volunteer for a shelter or rescue group, offer to foster dogs. This is a program most shelters and rescues have where kind-hearted people let dogs into their homes until they find their forever homes. Please do not add to the issue by getting a dog then realizing it doesn't fit your life and schedule – this only leads to neglect, stress, anxiety, and countless pets ending up at over-crowded shelters, never to make it out.

My Pitspective?

When it comes to pit bulls, everyone has an opinion — whether you have one, had one, met one or have only heard of them on the news, chances are, you have an opinion. Pits are fit, energetic dogs. Despite their athletic prowess, they are extremely affectionate by nature and provide their owners with endless love and their clownish personalities and comical expressions keep us constantly entertained. Many countless pits have been in and out of my life and house over the years. I typically describe them as the Ferraris of the dog world. By this I mean they are a high performance breed.

When they started out in the UK, as Staffordshire Bull Terriers, these dogs were known to be nanny dogs. This nickname came about because these dogs were typically found with kids in a daycare environment while the parents worked in mines. Chosen for their temperament around kids and terrier toughness, this breed was then exploited in another area — dog fighting. For many years pits were seen as the all-American family pet known for its loyalty and heroism. In this arena, the pit bull flourished. Later, however, pits were exploited for their best traits. Often becoming vilified by the media, pits became the number one dog to hate, thus filling local animal shelters.

For many years pits were the most respected and beloved of all American dogs. In fact, one particular pup, named Stubby, was the most decorated dog during World War One, earning the rank of sergeant and receiving two medals — one for warning about a gas attack and the other for holding a German spy captive until troops arrived. During one wartime campaign a poster was created featuring a dog representing each Allied army. Any guesses what breed stood tall for the United States? That's right – a Pit Bull. In both 1915 and 1917, Life Magazine touted the Pit Bull as America's dog on its cover and in 1929 Pete the Pit Bull became a household name due to his role on The Little Rascals and the Our Gang comedy series.

However, pockets of underground dog fighting began tearing down the image of the Pit as America's hero and slowly but surely replaced it with still images of vicious dogs attacking each other. This, of course, created a media monster – perpetuating the downfall of the Pit's reputation. Any negative story was beamed into our living rooms of bad people with bad dogs. Myths were born about lockjaw and indiscriminate killers. Gang members paraded dogs around with menacing abandon. Soon the war hero dog had become the dog to hate and fear. The New York Post ran a story about a man who was bitten badly on the leg by a dog of a different breed. He contacted the local media and told them but nobody found it interesting enough to report. As a little social experiment he allegedly called back a few days later with the same story but claimed his attacker was a pit bull. Three television stations and four newspapers sent reporters to get the scoop. This type of hysteria has even caused city bans on the breed, such as in Denver, Colorado. This type of sensationalized media cast Pit Bulls in the "mindless killing machine" light that the release of Jaws did to sharks.

Today's Pit Bulls, when treated correctly, are the same strong, energetic, reliable, loyal, and people-friendly dogs with a natural desire to please. Patient and good-natured with kids and often the class clown, these sturdy companions are equally game for roughhousing as they are for cuddle time. But be warned, a pit bull's tail vigorously wagging can easily clear a table or leave a welt on an unsuspecting leg!

Because of its fighting background, the tendencies towards animal aggression and selective social behavior can crop up. This breed can excite easily around other dogs they don't know or trust. However, this does not usually translate to humans. Often only wanting attention and praise from family members and strangers alike, pits are best placed with joyful, positive, and confident owners who love to exercise and command respect. Pits love to be with their owners as much as possible and make the perfect "sidekick dog."

Pits are a unique breed and aren't meant for everyone. Owners are held to a higher standard for both their sake and that of the breed's reputation. These dogs are often not dog social but rather are dog selective and wary of others. Pits are easily fired up and overly stimulated, especially around new dogs. They must have time to be properly introduced to new dogs in order to build trust.

In the right hands with the right training, the Pit Bull is a truly wonderful family pet. However, I often preach that Pits are not for everyone. Loyal and powerful, they are easily overstimulated and need an assertive owner who will implement the right structure and routine.

Remember, don't judge a dog by its cover – I have met countless docile, sweet pits and I've met just as many small dogs ready to bite at a moment's notice. At the end of the day it's all about knowing your own dog, acknowledging his limits, and recognizing his triggers.

With all dogs, communication is key. And while this stands true with pits, it's also extremely important to understand the breed itself. Whether you own a pit, love pits, admire them from afar, or are fearful of them due to popular misconceptions, I urge you to learn about this breed. Knowledge is crucial. Don't love or hate them for what you think they are. Get to know them, learn their distinguishing traits, and truly understand them. There is so much greatness within this breed – the loyalty, the silliness, the athleticism. They have so much to offer but because of overblown hype, they are truly the most misunderstood of all dogs out there.

If you own or are considering owning a pit, it's important to understand that you will be held to a different standard than other dog breed owners. Fair or not, this is the reality. You and your dog therefore become an ambassador for the breed.

So how does a pit owner deal with that? First off, don't exacerbate the problem by living up (or down) to the stereotype. It's similar to people profiling or being ignorant. Most people who have a preconceived prejudice against pit bulls have never actually met one. They are getting their information from sensationalized media stories. So change their view. Maybe they want to meet your well-behaved, friendly pit. Show your dog's good qualities and be understanding of the other person's view. Folks, in general, are scared of things they don't know or understand. I guarantee if they have a positive experience, they will tell others and they will question, if not completely change, their negative view of the breed.

But know your dog's limitations. If he isn't dog-friendly, then don't try anything risky. If you don't feel you have total control and you're not completely confident you'll have a positive experience, then avoid that situation. If asked why, simply say, "My dog is in training." If you give someone a negative experience, it will only reinforce what they already believe. And they will then tell even more people.

Put people at ease if you are confident in your dog's behavior. If a parent is uneasy about their child interacting with your dog, then reassure them. I have even asked parents in a tongue-and-cheek way, "Is your kid dog-friendly?" It can break the ice.

Rescuing a dog can be very rewarding, but getting to know that dog is key, especially if it's a pit bull. It's also essential to choose the right dog that fits your lifestyle and environment. It's all about temperament, temperament, temperament.

Many dogs at shelters and rescues have no real issues. It's a myth that these animals have been given up because they are problem dogs. Many of them lose their homes due to a foreclosure, change of living situation, divorce, or even because the owner passes away. Financial problems also play a large role in our homeless pet population. However, very often, a dog's behavior has no bearing on why he ends up at the shelter.

Simply put, pit bulls are wonderful dogs and, with the right training and commitment, are extremely rewarding to have and love. If you can't tell, I'm quite a fan of this breed and have two myself.

The Last Resort

Sometimes, after you've exhausted every option you can conjure up, you find yourself against a wall and it all boils down to a really, really tough decision. There are certain circumstances where rehoming a dog is the best option for everyone involved.

Peppo was a prime example of this. As an unemployed working dog living in the heart of Brentwood, Peppo was unhappy and restless. I felt his tension and anxiety the first time I met him. His owners initially called me in to help with his aggression issues, telling me he'd nipped at several members of their extended family. They adored their handsome border collie, but his behavior was becoming increasingly unpredictable, and with a new baby in the house, they needed to get Peppo reined in as soon as possible.

From the time I spent with Peppo and his family, over the course of several sessions, I quickly realized nobody was at fault. It was a simple case of personality clash. His owners were giving it their all, applying every trick and technique I threw at them. They changed their daily routine, accommodated his triggers, rearranged their home, purchased all the best training gear – all to no avail.

On the flip side, Peppo was not a bad dog. He was simply reacting to his environment. While his family bent over backwards to provide him the best home possible, they could not give him the one thing he needed – a life's purpose, aside from being a cuddle buddy. By nature, Peppo had trust issues and no matter what his parents tried, they simply couldn't break down that wall. Nature was overpowering nurture. Border collies are extremely smart and in order to feel secure and content, they need to be worked. Shockingly, there's not a great deal of livestock in need of herding in the middle of Los Angeles. To many, Peppo's cushy life in a Brentwood townhouse with loving parents would be the epitome of bliss. But for this high-strung fella, it was the root cause of his issues. Simply put, he needed a job. His family, on the other hand, was not hiring for any position other than that of a family pet; a companion. It boiled down to a simple case of irreconcilable differences.

Like with any relationship, when you're dealing with incompatibilities on this level, there is little either side can do to fix the problem. After all, you can't fit a square peg into a round hole, right? After giving Peppo's family my prognosis and advice, they made the difficult, but ultimately selfless, decision to find him a more fitting home. Rehoming a dog is a process in itself. You don't want to just run out and drop off your dog with the first person willing to take him in. And for most dog lovers, taking him to a shelter is a non-starter.

Peppo's family was committed to finding him his perfect home. As that dating site commercial says, do you want fast or forever? They wanted forever. If they couldn't provide Peppo with the environment he needed, then they'd make sure to find someone who could. So, what is the best way to rehome a dog? I'm glad you asked…

1. Get Your Dog Situated – In Peppo's case, his family was more than willing to keep him as long as it took to find him a home. This is not always possible, however. Judy, a long-time friend of mine, was terrified of dogs. It didn't matter how big or small, sweet or feisty. The mere sight of a dog sent her into a panic attack. This proved especially inconvenient when her mother passed away, leaving her in charge of Zoey – her mom's beloved fluffy little terrier mix. Because Zoey meant so much to her mother, Judy was determined to find her a wonderful home where she could happily continue to live her life. But for Judy, keeping Zoey at her own house was simply not an option. Knowing I work in the dog world and am constantly surrounded by dog people, Judy asked if I knew anyone who'd take care of Zoey until a forever home was found – and it just so happened I did. Offering to pay for foster care definitely helped expedite this process.

Obviously, if you're able to care for the dog until that perfect home is found, that's ideal. Dogs do best with structure, routine and stability. So, interrupting this as little as possible is preferred, but if you're in a position like Judy was, get creative and resourceful. First reach out to anyone familiar with the dog – like friends or family who've spent time around him. Make it clear you're not looking to just dump off the dog on them. Take a cue from Judy and sweeten the pot a bit. At the very least, you need to offer to pay for all the dog's expenses, like food, toys, bedding, medication, vet visits, etc. Taking in someone else's dog is generous enough, don't also stick them with the bill.

If the friends and family path leads to a dead-end, think outside the box. Sure, Judy and I were friends, but she also knew I had vast dog-related resources. Local shelters and rescues are great places to contact for help finding a foster. Typically, these types of organizations have great social media visibility and are always more than happy to help when it comes to an animal in need. Ask them to post a picture of your dog with a request for a foster on their various social media accounts. Again, find an incentive if need be.

Veterinarian offices, pet supply stores, grooming salons and any pet-related business are also good avenues. Ask to put up flyers requesting a foster. Bottom line, leave no stone unturned. Ensuring your dog has a safe, comfy and loving place to live temporarily is of the utmost importance. Not only because it's the right thing to do, but also to make sure he remains adoptable. If you stick him in a home where he's neglected or allowed to run amok, you'll find it even more difficult to rehome him. Which brings us to our next step…

2. Get Your Dog Up to Snuff – Before you really hit the ground running, you first need to rein in any blatantly bad behaviors your dog may exhibit. Clearly, there are certain things you cannot fix – else, he just might be the perfect dog for you. However, the better trained and behaved your dog, the easier it will be to find him that perfect home. Nobody wants to take on all your problems, am I right? If he's peeing on your rug, housebreak him. If he stares at you blankly when you say, "Sit," work on his basic commands. Don't worry too much about the more complicated issues. Like with Peppo, sometimes it's the environment, not the dog. So there's a good chance those bigger issues will diminish once he's in the right home for his personality.

3. Bio, Photos, & Videos – Now that you have your pup situated in a temporary foster home (be it yours or someone else's) and you're polishing those rough edges a bit, it's time to get to work. You will first need to write up a descriptive biography about your dog. Start with gender, age, breed, size, vaccination status, whether or not he's housebroken and neuter/spay information.

Be honest! Don't mark him as small and housebroken when he's actually a 90-pound peeing machine just because you think he'll find a home more easily. Sure, he may get adopted faster, but he'll also get returned to you just as quickly. Set him – and you – up to succeed, not to fail.

Once you've covered his basic stats, it's time to get creative; describe his likes, his dislikes, his activity level, quirks and any little trait that makes him unique and loveable.

The best bios are written in 1st person, from the dog's perspective – this adds an element of "Aw, how cute," that will get people's attention. Go onto rescue websites and peruse their postings for inspiration and ideas – most rescues have mastered the art of writing bios.

Put a positive spin on his less desirable behaviors. For example, if your dog can exhibit aggressive tendencies, word it as, "I need a strong owner." If your dog is hyperactive, consider saying, "I'd be perfect for an active hiker or jogger!"

Once you've conveyed his adorableness in words, it's camera time. Again, look through rescue postings to see how they photograph their dogs. Don't just snap a photo of him sleeping on his grungy dog bed. Try to get photos outdoors or in bright settings. Catch him when he's looking at you – potential adopters want to see that cute face of his. If you can capture him relaxed with his tongue hanging out, all the better. This makes him look like he's smiling. Dress him in scarves, bandanas, glasses, hats, reindeer antlers around Christmas, anything that makes him stand out and look as cute as possible. Don't underestimate the importance of great photos – they can really make or break the interest level you get. Think of it as online dating for dogs. Would you give a second look on Match to a blurry photo of a guy with his eyes closed? Would you message an expressionless girl who's barely looking at the camera? I think not.

The same goes for videos – take your dog outside and record him running around. Showcase his obedience abilities by making him sit, stay, and come. Capture him playing, chasing a stick, romping with other dogs — anything you can do to illustrate his cuteness and personality.

Carrie's a friend of mine who also dabbles in dog rescue – not formally, more by accident. Having several dogs of her own, Carrie frequently finds herself being the go-to person for strays in her neighborhood. A few years ago she found herself in possession of a tiny, 4-month-old Chihuahua/Min-Pin mix named Poppy. Poppy was ridiculously cute and Carrie knew she'd have little to no trouble finding her a great home. So, she did was any loving foster mom would do – she exploited Poppy's precious puppy personality to land her a new family. She flooded Poppy's adoption listing (which we'll get to in just a bit) with a cute bio and heartbreakingly hilarious and adorable photos and videos. Because Carrie had done this before, she knew there was a risk of people only wanting Poppy for her looks – which is not a good reason to adopt a dog. Sure, cuteness helps, but you want an adopter who loves your dog for who he is – not for his floppy ears or under bite. After all, looks fade, so you better make sure they like what's underneath. Carrie knew she needed to lure people in based on Poppy's cuteness then weed out potential adopters based on suitability. And that's exactly what she did. After a couple weeks and several "dates" with prospective owners, Poppy found a family who fell for her on every level. And they've been living happily ever after for the past 4 years.

4. Network– Now it's time to network, network, network. The more exposure your dog gets, the higher his odds of being seen by the right family. Reach out to everyone you know – friends, family, co-workers, neighbors, the bag boy at your local grocery store. Make flyers featuring his best photo, a quick list of his stats and your contact info. And then post them everywhere – telephone poles, veterinarian offices, pet supply stores. Most Starbucks have bulletin boards and will let you post flyers so long as you're not trying to sell your dog. Think outside the box and get to hangin'.

Reach out to local rescues, as they may have resources to help you. They can provide you with "Adopt Me" scarves and t-shirts your dog can don while on walks about town in high-traffic areas. Many rescue groups will also offer courtesy postings for dogs in search of homes on their websites and Facebook page. Ask about adoption events they host and whether or not you and your dog could make a cameo, upping his chances of being spotted by a prospective adopter. Your local shelters can also provide help – the key is to explore every channel possible. After all, you never know which one will pan out. One time an acquaintance snapped a photo of a dog I was rehoming for a friend. She happened to post it on SnapChat just for fun, but within a few minutes, she had a message from a friend asking about the dog. And wouldn't you know, that one random SnapChat led to a perfect match.

5. Post Your Pet – Let me begin by saying, I strongly advise against using Craigslist. This site is not a reputable space for posting adoptable dogs. Or for finding a date. There is no vetting process on either end and you can easily attract people who are up to no good. The key isn't finding your dog the quickest or easiest home – it's to find him the *right* home. PetFinder.com and Adopt-A-Pet.com are two really good ones; however, you have to be a rescue or shelter to post listings. This is another time when contacting rescue groups will come in very handy, as many will do this for you. Social media is also another treasure trove for posting your dog's bio, photos and videos – there are dozens and dozens of pages and groups out there specifically focused on helping dogs find new homes. Scour far and wide, high and low but if a certain site or person sends up any red flags, heed them. You'll be able to distinguish between those out there genuinely dedicated to helping animals from those out to make a quick buck. Beware of interest from people out-of-state. The logistics are a nightmare and you can't properly vet them due to the geographic barrier. They're what you call, "geographically undesirable." Check out the Instagram pages of rescue groups to see what hashtags they use for adoptable dogs. Be sure to also hashtag your city or area. Finding that perfect match for your dog is a numbers game – so do whatever you can to get as many eyes on him as possible. Just make sure they're the right eyes – no crazy eyes!

6. Application, Contract, & Move-In – I shouldn't have to say this but I will — it's crucial to vet potential adopters. Rescue groups utilize extensive adoption applications that ask myriad questions – anything from veterinary contact information and how many hours the pet will spend alone each day to what type of food the pet will eat and where he'll sleep – plus, everything in between. It's a good idea to review examples of adoption applications on rescue group websites to familiarize yourself with the best questions to ask. While some may seem a bit lengthy or invasive, the more specific questions – and the responses given – really do help give you a glimpse into that potential adopter's lifestyle and compatibility with your dog. You can even reach out to rescues for a general copy of their adoption application and adoption contract; then, modify it to you personally (i.e. change out their name and contact info with yours, remove or add questions, etc.). If someone refuses to fill out an application, take that as a huge red flag. Don't get desperate and just settle for someone. This is your dog, your process. Wait until you find someone willing to go through these steps. In my experience, desperation leads to the wrong home, which leads to a worse behaved dog coming back to you or losing the dog altogether. It all boils down to risk versus reward.

Once you've found someone seemingly suitable to your dog's needs, it's time to let them meet the dog. This will let you see how they interact and tell, to the best of your ability, whether they'll be a good match. Don't, however, let them leave with the dog that day. There are still a few steps to complete to ensure everybody is set up for success. Arrange the Meet & Greet in an environment where your dog is most comfortable and his true, relaxed personality will shine. And don't worry if you go through a few meet and greets without any results. This is very common. Sometimes it's them, sometimes it's you. Just be patient and don't get discouraged. Keep taking photos and videos to post, tweak the bio if need be. The Meet and Greet step can be lengthy, as this is the weeding out point. Just keep your head up and know the right home is out there. And don't worry, your dog doesn't realize he's being judged and scrutinized, so he's doing just fine. This process will be much harder on you than on him.

If you do find a love match, you'll then take one of two steps. You can either let the person foster-to-adopt – where they take the dog for a test run, so to speak. Or you can go on and finalize the adoption.

I always recommend, as it gives the new adopter and the dog a chance to experience day-to-day life together without a permanent commitment. If you choose this route, you'll want to have the adopter sign a foster contract – essentially, this contract ensures the foster will care for the dog, but you still maintain all legal rights to him. This gives you the power to swoop in and make any necessary decisions or changes on the dog's behalf.

Once you're ready to finalize the adoption, go on and make it as official as possible – and the best way to do this is with…can you guess? That's right — a contract! Think of it as a pre-nup. A pre-pup, if you will. Adoption contracts lay out your expectations and the responsibilities of the new owner. If you're unsure what should be included in the contract, I advise, once again, to do a little research. This type of documentation will hold all parties accountable and further aid in ensuring your dog is going to the best home possible. I also advise that there always be an adoption fee – even if it's only $100. You want to make sure the prospective adopter understands bringing in a dog is a commitment – on many levels, including financial. Basically, you want to make sure he's both willing and able to fork over a little dough for his new best friend. Shallow, I know, but it's a great vetting tool. You want to know the new adopter's got a little skin in the game.

Now that the ink is dry and the check cleared, it's move-in day. I advise against merely letting the new adopter pick up the dog and take him straight home. It's important that either you, or whoever has been caring for the dog, participates in the transition process. After all, your dog has been through so much – all those photos and bandanas, people rejecting him, others only liking him for his bod. He's over it already – don't just toss him in the deep end of the pool. Having someone he knows with him will put him more at ease as he enters his new home. Plus, it not only gives you a chance to scope out the new owner's house and rifle through his drawers, but it's also a final opportunity to instill any knowledge or advice you may have pertaining to your dog. Anything you can do to ease everyone in is great – maybe take along his favorite toy, dog bed, blanket, something he recognizes and that smells like him. This can help calm his nerves and help him to associate this new home with his old, familiar one. While moving him in, look around for anything you see that could cause issues – maybe a garbage can ripe for tipping over or a pair of shoes just asking to be chewed. Check out the height of the fence and make sure there are no holes – the last thing you want is for your dog to escape his new home and land in the pound. This is the time to provide both the new owner and your dog the tools for success. After all, the last thing anyone wants is another upheaval in your dog's home life.

I always advise having a trainer with you on move-in day to help set up everyone for success. Though you do know your dog best, a trainer can aid in answering more complex, behavioral questions, assessing the situation – both potential issues with the home and new owner – and can provide additional tools, advice and warnings that may slip your mind. The trainer can also act as the new owner's go-to person during this time of transition.

But always remember, YOU are your dog's best advocate, so go with your gut. The right home is out there, have faith in that and settle for nothing less.

7. Check-In – Once your dog is now in his new home, make yourself a resource. Check in via text or a call after his first night to see how things went. Let his new owners know you're there to provide support and answer questions. Don't just drop him off and vanish. As I've said several times, you know your dog best, so anything you can do to help the new owners will increase the chances of him not returning to you. But remember, you are no longer the owner; respect your dog's new family and be aware not to step on any toes or overstep a boundary.

Rehoming a dog is rarely an easy decision. Like with any relationship, we always want it to work out. We have high hopes, dreams of our future life together, images of growing old snuggled on the couch. But sometimes things go pear-shaped. I only advise rehoming after you've exhausted all other options. Though I've neatly summed it up in this chapter, it's not as easy as it sounds. I know people who've spent years waiting for that perfect home for their dog. But if you do it right, stay patient and diligent, you can find that perfect match for your dog. As with Peppo, who ended up finding a home on a ranch outside of San Diego. He lives with three other border collies and spends his days working, herding and fulfilling his purpose in life. He's content and secure, comfortable in his role within his new pack – both four and two-legged. Sometimes all it takes is a change of scenery to prove that one man's problem dog is another's best bud.

Disclaimer: These are the methods I have successfully used to rehome dogs; they may not work in every situation. This should be taken strictly as advice.